THE SYMBOLIC CONSTRUCTION OF COMMUNITY

A. P. COHEN
Department of Social Anthropology
University of Manchester

ELLIS HORWOOD LIMITED
Publishers · Chichester

TAVISTOCK PUBLICATIONS
London and New York

First published in 1985 by
ELLIS HORWOOD LIMITED
Market Cross House, Cooper Street
Chichester, Sussex, PO19 1EB, England
and

TAVISTOCK PUBLICATIONS LIMITED
11 New Fetter Lane, London EC4P 4EE

Published in the USA by
TAVISTOCK PUBLICATIONS
and ELLIS HORWOOD LIMITED
in association with METHUEN INC.
733 Third Avenue, New York, NY 10017

British Library Cataloguing in Publication Data
Cohen, Anthony P.
The symbolic construction of community. —
(Ellis Horwood series in key ideas)
1. Community
I. Title
307   HM131

ISBN 0−85312−933−9 (Ellis Horwood Ltd − Library Edn.)
ISBN 0−85312−855−3 (Ellis Horwood Ltd − Student Edn.)

Typeset by Ellis Horwood Limited
Printed in Great Britain by R. J. Acford, Chichester

Contents

ANTHONY PAUL COHEN has been Lecturer in Social Anthropology at the University of Manchester since 1979. He first joined Manchester as Lecturer in Sociology in 1971, having previously been Assistant Professor at Queen's University, Kingston, Ontario, and Research Fellow with the Institute of Social and Economic Research, Memorial University of Newfoundland, Canada.

A graduate of the University of Southampton with a B.A. in Philosophy and Politics (1967), an M.S. in Sociology and Politics (1968), and a Ph.D. for his thesis on Political Anthropology (1973), Dr. Cohen is the author of two previous books, as well as numerous papers and articles in scholarly journals and symposia. He is a Fellow of the Royal Anthropological Institute, a committee member of the Association of Social Anthropologists, and a member of the Rural Economy and Society study group.

Editor's Foreword

The concept of community has been one of the most compelling and attractive themes in modern social science, and at the same time one of the most elusive to define. It is in some ways tempting to view the recent attempts of some schools of Western sociology to announce the 'end' of community as a symptom of irritability with the unending definitional tangles created by this apparently elegant but infuriatingly slippery notion. Perhaps such a response is hardly surprising when one remembers that even as early as the mid-1950s an enterprising American sociologist had uncovered more than 90 discrete definitions of the term in use within the social sciences. Such enviable dexterity with the card-index could be discounted as grist to the scholarly mill were it not for the remarkable hold that the idea of community exerts over both the intellectual and popular mind. For whilst the conceptual ashes of community were being offered to the wind by sociologists and anthropologists of a radical or structuralist disposition, people throughout the Western world in modern industrialized societies were aggressively asserting their locality and ethnicity, their membership of *communities* which were real enough for them if not for those who ought to be studying them.

Community is, then, one of the *Key Ideas* of the social sciences, whether as a concept to be employed in the study of human societies or as an ideological notion which diverts attention away from the hard and large-scale forces which control peoples' lives — as Richard Sennett has expressively termed it, 'destructive gemeinschaft'. The concept — if for a moment we may be allowed to describe it as such — provides both a means of encompassing a wide variety of social processes and an idea which has much more than simply *technical* meaning, for it refers to symbols, values and ideologies which have popular currency. People manifestly *believe* in the notion of community, either as ideal or reality, and sometimes as both simultaneously. Now, as the American sociologist W. I. Thomas observed, if people believe a thing to be real, then it is real in its consequences for them. This duality of the concept is at the heart of the conceptual confusion to which it gives rise. The reality of 'community spirit', the sense of belonging which people exhibit to a small-scale social and cultural entity which is bigger than the 'family' but yet less impersonal than the bureaucracy or work organization, has sat uneasily alongside the attempts of sociologists and anthropologists to locate a structural dimension to *communitas*. This duality has also been overlain by a veneer of evaluative and ideological elements — community as 'normative prescription' has all too frequently interfered with 'empirical description' to the extent that a systematic sociology of community has proved to be impossible to construct.

The 'core' or *key* nature of the idea or concept of community reflects, then, both an undercurrent of social process and cultural meaning which is constantly present in modern societies, and a perennial problem for social science. Community continues to be of both a practical and an ideological significance to most people, and is thus an important area of study for the social sciences — despite prognostications to the contrary by those who see in the concept something which obscures the all-important structural dimension of class in social action. The study of community will continue to be necessary as long as local relationships play an important part in peoples lives, for we have a long way to go until we are all part of a McLuhanesque 'global village', or feel that the only determining feature of our social lives is our relationship to the means of production and membership of a social class.

Anthony Cohen's book on the Symbolic Construction of Community is the first in the series of volumes on *Key Ideas* in the social sciences, and it is fitting that the series should begin by focusing on a theme of such classic proportions. His book is an argument for the continued centrality of *community* as a key concept of the social sciences, uniting as it does sociology and social anthropology, His concern is not to rehash the stale debates about structural definitions of *Gemeinschaft,* nor to situate the study of communities in a context which subordinates localism or ethnicity to macro-social forces such as class, rationalization or universalism. Rather, he sets out to deal with community as it is symbolically constructed, as a system of values, norms, and moral codes which provides a sense of identity within a bounded whole to its members. This emphasis on *meaning* neatly sidesteps the definitional problems posed by the search for a structural model of community as a specific form of social organization. It demonstrates that structures do not, in themselves, create meaning for people and thus provides an effective answer to the question of why so many of the organizations designed to create 'community' as palliatives to anomie and alienation are doomed to failure.

Dr. Cohen provides much in the way of case-study material to illustrate the stages of his argument, and covers a wide range of examples to demonstrate the centrality of the symbolic dimension of community as its defining characteristic. These examples, culled from a marvellous range of ethnographic and sociological studies of specific communities, speak eloquently of the diversity of structural forms within which a sense of belonging to a *local* social context occur. Rather than being the sign of a traditional and outmoded social structure, the cultural experience of community as a bounded symbolic whole is something virtually universal in both non-industrial *and* industrial societies, transcending even the macro-social forces of capitalism and socialism in their many variations.

In focusing on the symbolic dimension of community, Dr. Cohen offers a way out of the impasse created by the search for a structurally-based definition, one which has created the impression that community is a uniquely 'traditional' social relationship, to be contrasted with the social forms of the 'modern' — exemplified by the impersonal, urbanized, rationalized, and class-based social structures of industrial society. As Dr. Cohen concludes, the issue to be faced in the study of community is not whether its structural limits have withstood the onslaught of social change, but whether its members are able to infuse its culture with vitality, and to construct a symbolic community which provides meaning and identity.

Peter Hamilton
February 1985

1
Introduction

SYMBOLISM AND BOUNDARY

'Community' is one of those words — like 'culture', 'myth', 'ritual', 'symbol' — bandied around in ordinary, everyday speech, apparently readily intelligible to speaker and listener, which, when imported into the discourse of social science, however, causes immense difficulty. Over the years it has proved to be highly resistant to satisfactory definition in anthropology and sociology, perhaps for the simple reason that all definitions contain or imply theories, and the theory of community has been very contentious. At its most extreme, the debate has thrown up ideologically opposed propositions which are equally untenable. For example, it used to be claimed that modernity and community are irreconcilable, that the characteristic features of community cannot survive industrialization and urbanization. It is a spurious argument for its opposition of 'community' and 'modernity' rests only upon ascribing stipulatively to community those features of social life which are supposed, by definition, to be lacking from modernity! Moreover, it is an argument which unjustifiably claims the authority of such seminal scholars as Durkheim, Weber, Tönnies and Simmel — unjustifiably because, as I shall argue, it perpetrates a misinterpretation, or highly selective reading, of these earlier writers. Others have suggested that the domination of modern social life by the state, and the essential confrontation of classes in capitalist society, have made 'community' a nostalgic, bourgeois and anachronistic concept. Once again, the argument is based entirely upon a highly particularistic and sectarian definition. However, its redundancy can be claimed not only on philosophical grounds, but also as being evident in the massive upsurge of community consciousness — in such terms as ethnicity, localism, religion, and class itself — which has swept the 'modern' world in recent years.

There is no attempt made in this book to formulate yet another definition. Rather, it is proposed to follow Wittgenstein's advice and seek not lexical meaning, but *use*. A reasonable interpretation of the word's use would seem to imply two related suggestions: that the members of a group of people (a) have something in common with each other, which (b) distinguishes them in a significant way from the members of other putative groups. 'Community' thus seems to imply simultaneously both similarity and difference. The word thus expresses a *relational* idea: the opposition of one community to others or to other social entities. Indeed, it will be argued that the use of the word is only occasioned by the desire or need to express such a distinction. It seems appropriate, therefore, to focus our examination of the nature of community on the element which embodies this sense of discrimination, namely, the *boundary*.

By definition, the boundary marks the beginning and end of a community. But why is such marking necessary? The simple answer is that the boundary encapsulates the identity of the community and, like the identity of an individual, is called into being by the exigencies of social interaction. Boundaries are marked because communities interact in some way or other with entities from which they are, or wish to be, distinguished (see Barth, 1969). The manner in which they are marked depends entirely upon the specific community in question. Some, like national or administrative boundaries, may be statutory and enshrined in law. Some may be physical, expressed, perhaps, by a mountain range or a sea. Some may be racial or linguistic or religious. But not all boundaries, and not *all* the components of *any* boundary, are so objectively apparent. They may be thought of, rather, as existing in the minds of their beholders. This being so, the boundary may be perceived in rather different terms, not only by people on opposite sides of it, but also by people on the same side.

We are talking here about what the boundary means to people, or, more precisely, about the meanings they give to it. This is the *symbolic* aspect of community boundary and, in so far as we aspire to understand the importance of the community in people's experience, it is the most crucial. To say that community boundaries are largely symbolic in character is, though, not merely to suggest that they imply different meanings for different people. It also suggests that boundaries perceived by some may be utterly imperceptible to others. For example, when the 1974–79 Labour Government formulated proposals for governmental devolution to Wales and Scotland, it did so on the apparent premise that there was sufficient unanimity of attitude within each of these entities to give particular legal expression to their boundaries. But such an assumption proved to be quite unjustified. The argument went very much further than whether devolution was, or was not a good thing, or whether this power or that discretion should or should not be devolved to the new authorities. Rather, it caused people *within* these entities to question whether the boundaries as envisaged by Whitehall were those most salient to them. The question became not simply, 'Are the Scots different from the English?', but, 'How different am I, as a particular Scot, from him, another particular Scot?' In other words, is the boundary dividing Scotland from England more meaningful to the highlander than those which distinguish him from the lowlander, the Glaswegian from the Edinburghian; the Shetlander from the Orcadian; the inhabitants of one Shetland island from those of another; the members of one township of a Shetland island from the members of another. As one goes 'down' the scale so the 'objective' referents of the boundary become less and less clear, until they may be quite invisible to those outside. But also as you go 'down' this scale, they become more important to their members for they relate to increasingly intimate areas of their lives or refer to more substantial areas of their identities.

Moreover, it is as one descends the scale that one approaches 'community' as something more than a rhetorical figment. When government leaders refer to the Common Market as a 'community', they may be regarded as indulging in rhetoric: stating an aspiration to common interest which is all too obviously missing in reality. But when the inhabitants of a Shetland island talk of 'their community', they refer to an entity, a reality, invested with all the sentiment attached to kinship, friendship, neighbouring, rivalry, familiarity, jealousy, as they inform the social process of everyday life. At this level, community is more than oratorical abstraction: it hinges crucially on consciousness.

This consciousness of community is, then, encapsulated in perception of its boundaries, boundaries which are themselves largely constituted by people in interaction. It is in part this process, the symbolic constitution of boundaries, that is referred to in the title of this book.

But, in addition to recognizing the symbolic constituents of community consciousness, we have also to reveal the essentially symbolic nature of the idea of community itself, again essentially enshrined in the concept of boundary.

Boundaries enclose elements which may, for certain purposes and in certain respects, be considered to be more like each other than they are different. But they also mark off these elements from those which differ. In this regard, the boundaries of communities perform the same function as do the boundaries of all categories of knowledge. If we extract from this total cognitive stock a sub-genus, categories of *social* knowledge, we find that all such categories are marked by symbolism (see Needham, 1979). The symbolism may be explicit as, for example, in rituals which discriminate among roles, between life and death, between stages and statuses in the life cycle, between gender, between generations, between the pure and the polluted. It may be explicit in the arcane fantasy of myth and totem. But much of our symbolism does not have a special vocabulary or idiomatic behaviour: it is, rather, part of the meaning which we intuitively ascribe to more instrumental and pragmatic things in ordinary use — such as words. Philosophers have long since drawn our attention to the capacity of language to express attitude as well as to denote object. In Cranston's examples, words such as 'freedom' and 'democracy' do not merely describe forms of government and legal status. they also tell us how to regard these forms. They are 'hurrah' words, as opposed to 'boo' words (Cranston, 1954). The anthropologist, Mary Douglas, similarly shows that the use of the word 'dirt' does rather more than signify the particles which lie under the finger nail: it also expresses an attitude, 'ugh!', and prescribes a remedy, 'scrub!' (Douglas, 1966).

Symbols, then, do more than merely stand for or represent something else. Indeed, if that was all they did, they would be redundant. They also allow those who employ them to supply part of their meaning. If we refer again to the examples of categories mentioned above, age, life, father, purity, gender, death, doctor, are all symbols shared by those who use the same language, or participate in the same symbolic behaviour through which these categories are expressed and marked. But their meanings are *not* shared in the same way. Each is mediated by the idiosyncratic experience of the individual. When I think about 'fatherhood', my reflections on paternity in general are informed by *my* experience of *my* father and of *my* children. Where I a Scot voting in the devolution referendum, I should not merely mave measured myself against the English, but would refract 'Scottishness' through my personal experience — as Shetland fisherman, Kincardine farmer,

Fife miner or Clydeside shipbuilder, father, son, brother, agnostic, music lover, socialist, and so forth. Symbols do not so much express meaning as give us the capacity to make meaning.

Not *all* social categories are so variable in meaning. But those whose meanings are the most elusive, the hardest to pin down, tend to be those also hedged around by the most ambiguous symbolism. In these cases the content of the categories is so unclear that they exist largely or only in terms of their symbolic boundaries. Such categories as justice, goodness, patriotism, duty, love, peace, are almost impossible to spell out with precision. The attempt to do so invariably generates argument, sometimes worse. But their *range* of meanings can be glossed over in a commonly accepted symbol – precisely because it allows its adherents to attach their own meanings to it. They share the symbol, but do not necessarily share its meanings. Community is just such a boundary-expressing symbol. As a symbol, it is held in common by its members; but its meaning varies with its members' unique orientations to it. In the face of this variability of meaning, the consciousness of community has to be kept alive through manipulation of its symbols. The reality and efficacy of the community's boundary – and, therefore, of the community itself – depends upon its symbolic construction and embellishment. This essay discusses some of the features most commonly associated with this process.

SYMBOLISM AND MEANING

'If you live in Shinohata', wrote Ronald Dore, 'the "outside world" begins three hundred yards down the road . . .' (Dore, 1978, p. 60). We do not have to construe community just in terms of locality, but more properly, in the sense which Dore expresses so lucidly and describes with such affectionate evocation of the Japanese village he studied at intervals for twenty-five years: the sense of a primacy of belonging. Community is that entity to which one belongs, greater than kinship but more immediately than the abstraction we call 'society'. It is the arena in which people acquire their most fundamental and most substantial experience of social life outside the confines of the home. In it they learn the meaning of kinship through being able to perceive *its* boundaries – that is, by juxtaposing it to non-kinship; they learn 'friendship'; they acquire the sentiments of close social association and the capacity to express or otherwise manage these in their social relationships. Community, therefore, is where one learns and continues to practice how to 'be social'. At the risk of substituting one indefinable category for another, we could say it is where one acquires 'culture'.

Learning to be social is not like learning grammar or the Highway Code. It is not reducible to a body of rules. Of course, one can identify rule-like principles in culture. Thus, for example, we can say that the Temne of Sierra Leone reserve the right hand to upper bodily behaviour; the left, to cope with the lower body (Littlejohn, 1972). We could make a similarly generalized statement in suggesting that the Whalsay Islanders of Shetland avoid open dispute or the public assertion of opinion (Cohen, 1977). These 'principles' are sufficiently observed in practice that their contravention would identify the perpetrator as outsider or as deviant. They differ from more objective rules, however, in that they are not associated unambiguously, nor even obviously, with a fixed and shared rationale. The Temne might well discriminate between left- and right-handedness, but this is not to say that they all do so for the same reason, nor for any 'conscious' reason, nor that they would accept the interpretations of their behaviour offered by Littlejohn's supposedly authoritative informant. People attach their own meanings to such prescriptions and proscriptions. In this respect, they are less *rules* of society than its symbols. Thus, when we speak of people acquiring culture, or learning to be social, we mean that they acquire the symbols which will equip them to be social.

This symbolic equipment might be compared to vocabulary. Learning words, acquiring the components of language, gives you the capacity to communicate with other people, but does not tell you *what* to communicate. Similarly with symbols: they do not tell us *what* to mean, but give us the capacity to make meaning. Culture, constituted by symbols, does not impose itself in such a way as to determine that all its adherents should make the same sense of the world. Rather, it merely gives them the capacity to make sense and, if they tend to make a similar kind of sense it is not because of any deterministic influence but because they are doing so with the same symbols. The quintessential referent of community is that its members make, or believe they make, a similar sense of things either generally or with respect to specific and significant interests, and, further, that they think that that sense may differ from one made elsewhere. The reality of community in people's experience thus inheres in their attachment or commitment to a common body of symbols. Much of the boundary-maintaining process we shall look at later is concerned with maintaining and further developing this commonality of symbol. But it must again be emphasized that the sharing of symbol is not necessarily the same as the sharing of meaning.

People's experience and understanding of their community thus resides in their orientation to its symbolism. It will be clear, then, that a crucial step for us in attempting to unravel analytically the concept of community must involve some further discussion of the relations among symbolism, culture and meaning.

In what has become one of the most celebrated statements in recent anthropological writing, Geertz proclaims, '. . . man is an animal suspended in webs of significance he himself has spun . . .'. These webs constitute 'culture', whose analysis is, '. . . not an experimental science in search of law but an interpretive one in search of meaning' (1975a, p. 5). There are three interrelated and powerful principles contained within Geertz's precise and eloquent formulation. The first is that culture ('webs of significance') is created and continually recreated by people through their social interaction, rather than imposed upon them as a Durkheimian body of social fact or as Marxist superstructure. Secondly, being continuously in process, culture has neither deterministic power nor objectively identifiable referents ('law'). Third, it is manifest, rather, in the capacity with which it endows people to perceive meaning in, or to attach meaning to social behaviour. Behaviour does not 'contain' meaning intrinsically; rather, it is found to be meaningful by an act of interpretation: we 'make sense' of what we observe. The sense we make is 'ours', and may or may not coincide with that intended by those whose behaviour it was. Thus, in so far as we 'understand' the behaviour which goes on around us and in which we participate, we make and act upon interpretations of it: we seek to attach meaning to it. Social interaction is contingent upon such interpretation; it is, essentially, the transaction of meanings.

Interpretation implies a substantial degree of what, *faute de mieux*, we must call 'subjectivity'. When it is a feature of social interaction, subjectivity clearly suggests the possibility of imprecision, of inexactitude of match, of ambiguity, of idiosyncracy. In other words, different people oriented to the same phenomenon are likely to differ from each other in certain respects in their interpretations of it. They may not be aware of this difference, especially if the phenomenon is a common feature of their lives. Their disagreement is not necessarily, then, an impediment to their successful interaction. Indeed, often the contrary is the case. People can find common currency in behaviour whilst still tailoring it subjectively (and interpretively) to their *own* needs.

These interpretations are not random. They tend to be made within the terms characteristic of a given society, and influenced by its language, ecology, its traditions of belief and ideology, and so forth. But neither are they immutable. They are, rather, responsive to the circumstances of interaction, both among individuals, and between the society as a whole and those across its boundaries. The vehicles of such interpretations are symbols. By their very nature symbols permit interpretation and provide scope for interpretive manoeuvre by those who use them. Symbols are often defined as things 'standing for' other things. But they do not represent these 'other things' unambiguously: indeed, as argued above, if they did so they would be superfluous and redundant. Rather, they 'express' other things in ways which allow their common form to be retained and shared among the members of a group, whilst not imposing upon these people the constraints of uniform meaning. Because symbols are malleable in this way, they can be made to 'fit' the circumstances of the individual. They can thus provide media through which individuals can experience and express their attachment to a society without compromising their individuality. So versatile are symbols they can often be bent into these idiosyncratic shapes of meaning without such distortions becoming visible to other people who use the same symbol at the same time.

Consider the following symbol as an example: ⊕. On any demonstration or procession at which this symbol is prominently displayed, sympathizers could all comfortably associate themselves with it and, indeed, find it an adequate expression of their position for the purposes of a certain kind of discourse. Yet, were they to debate among themselves the merits of unilateralism as opposed to multilateralism; the advisability of one kind of compaigning strategy as opposed to another; their attitude towards NATO or to the Soviet bloc; the importance of Christianity, pacifism or socialism to their support for nuclear disarmament, the simple symbol would become revealed as an effective, but very superficial gloss upon an enormous variety of opinion, much of it hostile rather than merely opposed. This is not just to say that any great social movement is invariably a coalition of interests. It also demonstrates the versatility of symbols: people of radically opposed views can find their own meanings in what nevertheless remain common symbols.

This example is of a very particular kind of symbol: it is, essentially, an emblem, a sign. Most symbols do not have visual or physical expression but are, rather, ideas. This may make their meanings even more elusive.

A recent study of the community of Elmdon, near Cambridge, examines the variable meanings which association with the village has for different categories of its inhabitants. To some, 'village' designates place, discriminating it from other communities and, in particular, from the larger towns. To others, those who judge themselves to be 'Real Elmdoners', it connotes kinship and class. Here, it is appropriate to consider the 'idea of villageness' as symbolic and, again, it is noticeable that it renders eloquent but different meanings for its various users (see Strathern, 1981; 1982a and b). Similarly, David Schneider shows that a kinship system like that which predominates in the United States – which, by comparison with others, might appear to be rather prosaic and attenuated – must be understood not as a system of '. . . roles and relationships which Americans can be observed to undertake in their day-to-day behaviour in situations of family life . . .', but, rather, as a system of symbols: as a set of named boxes to be filled with people's experience (Schneider, 1980). There is no necessary uniformity between the categories symbolically marked, say, 'uncle,' 'cousin' and the meanings attached to them. Or, to put it another way, the biogenetic and affinal relationships named in a kinship system do not exhaust the meanings attached to them, any more than does the civic status of Elmdon exhaust the meanings with which its residents invest their village.

Now, it has long been recognized that communities are important repositories of symbols, whether in the forms of totems, football teams or war memorials. All of these are like the categories of a kinship system: they are symbolic markers of the community which distinguish it from other communities. However, the argument being advanced here is somewhat different. It is that the community itself and everything within it, conceptual as well as material, has a symbolic dimension, and, further, that this dimension does not exist as some kind of consensus of sentiment. Rather, it exists as something for people 'to think with'. The symbols of community are mental constructs: they provide people with the means to make meaning. In so doing, they also provide them with the means to express the particular meanings which the community has for them.

Everything, therefore, may be grist to the mill of symbolism. Moreover, the reality of community in the lives of its members, like that of 'kinship' in Schneider's account of Chicagoans, is symbolic. The same must also necessarily be true of its boundary. The sea may divide one island from another, just as the parish border may mark the beginning and end of a settlement. But these boundaries are symbolic receptacles filled with the meanings that members impute to and perceive in them. Much of the symbolic behaviour we will discuss later is concerned with the generation of such meaning and its investment in the boundary.

SYMBOL, CULTURE, COMMUNITY

It will be clear from the foregoing discussion that in this book the community is not approached as a morphology, as a structure of institutions capable of objective definition and description. Instead, we try to understand 'community' by seeking to capture members' experience of it. Instead of asking, 'what does it look like to us? What are its theoretical implications?, we ask, 'What does it appear to mean to its members?' Rather than describing analytically the form of the structure from an external vantage point, we are attempting to penetrate the structure, to look *outwards* from its core.

The picture we have so far sketched of the community as a mêlée of symbol and meaning cohering only in its symbolic gloss contrasts sharply with earlier, and particularly functionalist, accounts. Durkheim's central and abiding concern was with solidarity, with the contrivance of bonds that could link indissolubly the members of society. The ideal form he proposes for an economically differentiated society is one modelled on the division of labour, in which different functions are harnessed in a productive whole. The points of difference which divide people are transformed instead into the linchpins of interdependency which unite them. The Durkheimian aspiration is to integration. Later writers treated culture as just such an integrating force. Parsons even uses the very term 'integration' to label the taxonomic box he reserves to culture. In the same tradition, Arensberg and Kimball developed a theory of community in which integration was the key factor and supreme function (Arensberg & Kimball, 1965 p. ix). The version of culture which emerges from this 'integrative' tradition is one which treats it as something held in common by the members of a society: 'a way of thinking, feeling, believing . . .' (Kluckhohn, 1962, p. 25). Yet, the foregoing argument has suggested that what is actually held in common is not very substantial, being *form* rather than content. Content differs widely among members. It follows, therefore, that insofar as community provides the context for culture, a different conception of it is required. We propose that rather than thinking of community as an *in*tegrating mechanism, it should be regarded instead as an *agg*regating device.

In this approach, then, the '*common*ality' which is found in community need not be a uniformity. It does not clone behaviour or ideas. It is a commonality of *forms* (ways of behaving) whose content (meanings) may vary considerably among its members. The triumph of community is to so contain this variety that its inherent discordance does not subvert the apparent coherence which is expressed by its boundaries. If the members of a community come to feel that they have less in common with each other than they have with the members of some other community then, clearly, the boundaries have become anomalous and the integrity of the 'community' they enclose has been severely impugned. The important thrust of this argument is that this relative similarity or difference is not a matter for 'objective' assessment: it is a matter of feeling, a matter which resides in the minds of the members themselves. Thus, although they recognize important differences among themselves, they also suppose themselves to be more like each other than like the members of other communities. This is precisely because, although the meanings they attach to the symbols may differ, they share the symbols. Indeed, their common ownership of symbols may be so intense that they may be quite unaware or unconcerned that they attach to them meanings which differ from those of their fellows. As we saw earlier, the symbol can function quite effectively as a means of communication without its meanings being rigorously tested. A courting couple may exchange an expression of sentiment:

> 'I love you!'
> '*I* love *you*!'

without feeling the need to engage in a lengthy and complicated disquisition on the meaning of the word 'love'. Yet it is, of course, a word which masks an extremely complex idea. So complex is it that were our two lovers to attempt to explain their meanings precisely they might well find themselves engaged in fierce argument.

Symbols are effective because they are imprecise. Though obviously not contentless, part of their meaning is 'subjective'. They are, therefore, ideal media through which people can speak a 'common' language, behave in apparently similar ways, participate in the 'same' rituals, pray to the 'same' gods, wear similar clothes, and so forth, without subordinating themselves to a tyranny of orthodoxy. Individuality and commonality are thus reconcilable. Just as the 'common form' of the symbol aggregates the various meanings assigned to it, so the symbolic repertoire of a community aggregates the individualities and other differences found within the community and provides the means for their expression, interpretation and containment. It provides the range within which individuality is recognizable (see Cohen, 1978). It continuously transforms the reality of difference into the appearance of similarity with such efficacy that people can still invest the 'community' with ideological integrity. It unites them in their opposition, both to each other, and to those 'outside'. It thereby constitutes, and gives reality to, the community's boundaries.

COMMUNITY: THE 'CLASSICAL' TRADITION, AND CHICAGO

Following the brief preview above of the argument to be presented in this book, let us take a similarly brief step backwards to place it more securely within the history of the debate about the meaning of community conducted by sociologists and anthropologists.

The scholars writing at the turn of the century, to whom we alluded earlier, were working within the then recent tradition of evolutionary theory. Social theorists had taken over from natural scientists the view that organisms become increasingly refined and well-adapted to changing circumstances. Darwin argued, of course, that those that could not thus develop would perish. Throughout the late nineteenth century, we find social theorists speculating upon the nature of the change required in *social* organisms to meet the contemporary conditions of the burgeoning processes of urbanization, industrialization, social and geographical mobility, and the greater heterogeneity which followed in the wake of these developments. Their speculations were frequently based on the contrast between two, apparently historically disjunctive, types of society. For example, Maine juxtaposes the society in which relationships are essentially ascriptive and founded, through blood-based rank order, on largely immutable hierarchies, with a 'later' evolved social form in which they are made with a degree of freedom and founded on legal agreement. The first he characterizes as 'status'; the latter, as 'contract'. The essential transformation effected in the transition from the first to the second is that kinship becomes less significant in constraining social action and defining the universe of a person's social relationships, and gives way to the 'individual'. Tönnies described a transition taking place between *'gemeinschaft'*, the society of intimacy, of close personal knowledge, of stability, and *gesselschaft,* a society characterized by ego-focused, highly specific and possibly discontinuous relationships, in which the individual interacts within different social milieux for different purposes. Durkheim dichotomized the types as, first, mechanical solidarity, the society founded upon likeness, and unable to tolerate dissimilarity (therefore unable to encompass anything more than a rudimentary division of labour), and, second, organic solidarity, the society founded upon the integration of difference into a collaborative, and therefore harmonious, complex whole. Here, again, the individual is a composite of specialized activities.

A common view running through these various approaches is that of individuals' social lives becoming more and more specialized, not just in their labour, but in all of their social relations. They engage with different people for different, and limited purposes. Their lives are thus led on a variety of levels — and, possibly, in different locations as well. They are therefore known to most others only in the terms in which they are brought into interaction with them — as client, as baker, as tax-collector, as priest and so forth. Except in relation to their most intimate associates, probably confined to their nuclear kin, the 'whole' social person is incongruent with modernity. They are become, rather legal entities, bit-part players on various social stages, roles. Behaviour in modernity has therefore to be modelled by the specific end in view; it has to be, as Weber rather regretfully observed, 'rational'. For Durkheim, such modelling has to take the form of structural regulation: the individual interests of the parts have to be subordinated by the irreducible whole. Anything less results in the pathology of normlessness, of de-regulation, of *anomie*.

The view is, then, that this transformation moves individuals from a social context where they are continually subjected to a regime composed of the largely indistinguishable components of kin, neighbours and peers, providing a milieu in which virtually their entire social lives are lived among people who constitute their total social universes, and in which they are known to each other fully and personally, to another, characterized by anonymity, by explicit and limited function, in which individuals have to weave their way among their different sets of relationships.

Not surprisingly, perhaps, the evolutionary heritage of these writers led commentators to see the transformations they described as being historical, as well as social. Moreover, they associated 'community' (treated as a quality of social life) with the former, now anachronistic mode, and regarded it as lacking, or as being very attenuated, in the latter. This view was further developed in the tradition of sociology and anthropology known as the Chicago School. Based initially on the pioneering urban studies of Robert Park, Ernest Burgess and, later, Louis Wirth, the school spawned a celebrated *oeuvre* of urban ethnography; and a powerful anthropological comparison of urban and rural life in Redfield's seminal work was continued by Horace Miner, Oscar Lewis, and others. This American tradition was overwhelmingly Durkheimian in orientation and certainly led to the conventional view that Maine, Durkheim, Weber, Tönnies and others were providing, essentially, theories of historical social change and development.

One may suppose that this reading of the 'classical' masters is based, in part, on the polemical nature of much of Durkheim's and Weber's work with regard to the need for reform in their own societies, and on their explicit concern with contemporary conditions. In part it may also derive from a felt need to oppose the comprehensive theory of historical process laid down by Marx, Engels, and later Marxist historians. Whilst it is not our task to engage in a critical analysis of this interpretation, it is appropriate for us to raise a qualification to it. Weber made perfectly clear that, true to his abiding sociological method, he was purveying accounts of essentially 'ideal' types: that is to say, analytic constructs lacking empirical analogues. Moreover, he was concerned with practicality: with *understanding* 'irrationality', not with excising it. Efficiency, the 'ethic of ultimate ends', must be tempered by, and married to, compassion, 'an ethic of responsibility'. These, he says, '. . . are not absolute contrasts but rather supplements . . ." (1948, p. 127).

Both Durkheim and Weber argued the *need* for change. But both were too astute and sensitive as observers of society to suppose that there could be any inevitability about its occurrence, nor any monolithic character to the social forms ushered in. Just as both achieved new heights in the sociological explanation of religion, whilst maintaining their own agnosticism; so they also mapped out with extraordinary prescience and clarity the social correlates of the capitalistic economy, without becoming apologists for it. Even though the influence of the evolutionary theorists, such as Fustel de Coulanges, is clearly evident in Durkheim's work, it is equally clear that he did not see mechanic and organic solidarities as historically incompatible, but, rather, as contrasted tendencies within society at any one time. Thus, while, like Rousseau, he calls for political structures which would generate a social spirit willing the general interest, he accepts that the obvious bases of these structures would be sectional interests, organized, for example, upon occupational associations. The two tendencies do not so much represent the archetypal modes of different historical eras which happen to coincide. Rather, they each speak, in Durkheim's view, of differences in the relationship of the individual to society — differences, therefore, in modes of social process. Mechanical solidarity is the aggregate of socially constituted individuals: 'society living and acting within us' (1964, p. 129). Organic solidarity is society constituted *by* individuals, where differences which distinguish them from each other become also the bases for their integration and collaboration in a solidary whole. It is a solidarity which 'is possible only if each one has a sphere of action which is peculiar to him; that is, a personality' (1964, p. 131). What he describes, then, are not two societies, or a society in different historical epochs; but, rather, two aspects of society at a given historical moment:

> In the first, what we call society is a more or less organized totality of beliefs and sentiments common to all the members of the group: this is the collective type. On the other hand, the society in which we are solidary in the second instance is a system of different, special functions which definite relations unite. These two societies really make up only one. They are

two aspects of one and the same reality . . . . (1964, p. 129).

Mechanical solidarities thus persist into societies which also manifest organicism. If we accept the conventional association of community with mechanic solidarity (without accepting it as an exclusive association!) then we may conclude that community persists within these complex social forms. Another writer also cites the passage quoted above to support his contention that mechanical solidarity is less an historical figment than it is a contrived symbolic expression of likeness — of commonality. It is a likeness in terms of limited and specific variables selected from a universe (the *organic* entity) of possible and available variables (Boon, 1982, pp. 54–5). In terms of the argument of this book, it is tantamount to the symbolic construction of boundary. In this alternative reading, then, community, and engagement in non-communal relations, are differing, but complementary modes of social life. Boon refers to their Durkheimian terms as 'two sides of the same coin' (1982, p. 63). Later, we shall return to this idea in its guise as 'complementary opposition' (see *infra,* pp. 115ff).

The complementarity of the two modes was, however, largely neglected by the Chicago scholars who used Durkheim's dichotomy as a paradigm for their own distinctions between urban and rural societies. In slightly later renderings, this distinction was presented as one graduated on a linear scale. But the earlier urban sociologists treated it as betokening an absolute difference in the quality of social life. Rural society ('community') was small, parochial, stable, and 'face-to-face': people interacted with each other as 'total' social persons informed by a comprehensive personal knowledge of each other, their relationships often underpinned by ties of affinity and consanguinity. It was a traditional and conservative way of life, in which people valued custom for its own sake and, given a reasonable degree of potential self-sufficiency in the production of their subsistence, felt substantially in control of their lives, subject, of course, to the vicissitudes of nature and the divine.

Urban life, it was suggested, was different in almost every respect. It required the mental reconditioning of the individual which, in the case of rural migrants must be affected by re-socialization. But the city person is really the product of a later evolutionary stage and is a rather more refined species of the genus than his rural cousins. 'The city', wrote Robert Park, 'is . . . the natural habitat of civilized man'. He goes on to quote Spengler to the effect that developed man is a city creature, and that, 'World history is the history of city men' (1925, p. 3). The individual in urban society lives his social life in a multiplicity of contexts, residing in one, working in another, travelling through still others, perhaps taking his leisure somewhere else altogether. This plurality of contexts is replicated structurally in the very ecology of the city, divided into separate zones ('zones of succession') clearly distinguishable by population and function. The vestiges of community are to be found only at the level of the neighbourhood. However, with the singular exception of the ghetto, these para-communities are only tenuous for the neighbourhood itself is undermined by its integration into the city's infrastructure, by social mobility (and, therefore, impermanence) and by the plurality of roles borne by its members (1925, pp. 9ff). The old communality of rural life is broken down by the division of specialized labour, and is replaced by a solidarity built upon interdependence — in effect, an organic relationship based on mutual self-interest (pp. 13–16) — but one informed by functionality, rather than by sentiment:

the growth of cities has been accompanied by the substitution of indirect, 'secondary', for direct, face-to-face 'primary' relations in the associations of individuals in the community. (p. 23)

He does recognize that the breakdown of these 'primary' associations produces its own problems of de-regulation, isolation, even crime, and that the attempts of the political machines to compensate for the 'pre-urban' primary agencies of socialization and control may be less than adequate.

The processes of segregation establish moral distances which make the city a mosaic of little worlds, which touch but do not interpenetrate. This makes it possible for individuals to pass quickly and easily from one moral milieu to another, and encourages the fascinating but dangerous experiment of living at the same time in several different contiguous, but otherwise widely separated worlds. (1925, pp. 40–1)

A little later, another writer in the same genre saw people coping with this fragmentation in their lives (the loss of community?) by adopting attitudes of reserve and indifference, '. . . as devices for immunizing themselves against the personal claims and expectations of others' (Wirth, 1951 (1938), p. 54). Social relations are kept impersonal:

our physical contacts are close but our social contacts are distant . . . We see the uniform which denotes the role of the functionaries and are oblivious to the personal eccentricities that are hidden behind the uniform. (1951, p. 55)

Again, we have the image of the individual threading an idiosyncratic route through a variety of disconnected social milieux, each claiming a different aspect of the self and functioning 'only with reference to a single segment of his personality' (p. 57).

Thus the structural determinism of this school of thought led its members to postulate a clear causal relationship between the fragmentation of social life in the city, and the fragmentation of the individual into a mere basket of roles. Rural and urban societies were treated in this tradition as the very antithesis of each other. Rural society, called by Redfield 'folk' society, was the contrary in every respect of the urban archetype, painted by Park, Wirth and others. Personalistic, traditionalistic, stable, religious, familial, it is the classical repository of community. The further one moves along Redfield's continuum from 'folk' to 'urban' society, the greater becomes the loss of community.

Again, a proper critique of this position is beyond the scope of this essay; in any case, critiques abound in the literature. (With particular respect to their application to later community studies, see, for example, Pahl, 1968; Bell and Newby, 1971.) Our concerns are, first, to note that although the argument shows a strong Durkheimian influence, it is actually unfaithful to his assertion of the complementarity of mechanical and organic solidarities. This is partly because it treats the transition between the types as an inexorable process of change which makes them historically incompatible, and partly because its determinism makes the nature of human association entirely a product of the dominant features of its structural context, such as size and scale. Arguably, also, it is psychologically naive, confusing the appearance of personal, role-based social behaviour, with its actuality – the incorporation of various roles by the personality. Thus, the fractionalization of the individual in virtue of the plurality of his roles is a figment of structural-functional analysis. The individual reconciles the multiplicity of the roles he plays; for example, a woman's experience as mother will also inform her performance as teacher or as doctor, and both would be part of her persona as friend. The various aspects of her behaviour are thus constituents of a greater whole, rather than mere discrete compartments of her ego (cf. Turner, 1962). Secondly, we may note that, as a consequence, it is irredeemably incorrect in postulating the end of community. Innumerable studies have shown us 'community' within the city. The history of community action over the last twenty-five years has reminded us, if we needed reminding, that people map out their social identities and find their social orientations among the relationships which are symbolically close to them, rather than in relation to an abstracted sense of society. Much like horses dunging out the

boundaries of their territory (if readers will forgive the prosaic metaphor), so people put down their social markers symbolically, using the
symbolic vocabulary which they can most comfortably assimilate to
themselves, and then contributing to it creatively. They thereby make
community. Whether or not people behave within the 'community'
mode, or in some more specialized and limited way, is less a matter of
structural determinism than of boundary management.

THE DEBRIS OF CHICAGO: SOME MYTHS EXPOSED

The theoretical emphasis in this essay is, then, on the ways in which
people contrive community and, in particular, on the resourcefulness
with which they use symbols in this regard to re-assert community and
its boundaries when the processes and consequences of change threaten
its integrity. In order to complete the scenario, it is desirable that we
attempt to disperse some of the sociological fog which has persistently
enshrouded the community.

(i) The myth of simplicity and the 'face-to-face' society

Throughout the Chicago tradition there is to be found the view that
urban society is, by definition, more complicated than that of the rural
community. The view was expressed in the taxonomic classification of
societies into 'simple' and 'complex', with somewhat misleading results.
The assumption is that a society in which a large number of people play
a range of highly specialized roles is somehow more complicated than
one in which a relatively small number of people play a similar, or even
larger variety of roles, some of them highly specialized, some of them
less so. One may legitimately wonder, 'complicated for whom?' The
distinction appears to be a quantitative one, assuming that complexity
varies proportionately with scale and the proliferation of institutions.
It pays scant regard to the qualitative dimensions of social life. For
those of us used to negotiating the everyday crises of life in metropolitan society, a slight disagreement with a taxi driver, perhaps about
the size of his tip, or with a lawyer, about the size of his bill, or with a
builder, about his workmanship, are matters which, though irritating,
we can usually take in our stride. They require us to settle the dispute
in some way or other, but we do not normally expect such incidents to
intrude upon the rest of our lives. But we may imagine that such
incidents are rather more difficult to deal with if they concern people
who also happen to be related to each other, or who will confront each
other repeatedly and frequently in the contexts of other activities. Both
the management of such relationships, and the discrimination among

the variety of activities they span, call for much more complicated strategies than merely walking out of the room, or beating a hasty retreat from an irate cabbie. It is, of course, in the smaller-scale social milieu of the community that we should expect to encounter the latter complexity.

In a taxonomy rather more sensitive to the differences between these kinds of relationships, Gluckman labels the first, single-stranded, highly specific relationship as 'simplex'; the second, multi-stranded, as 'multiplex'. It is tempting to associate the first with the impersonality of the 'secondary' relationships which, say Park, Redfield and the others, characterize urban, 'complex' society, and the second with 'primary', 'face-to-face' relationships of the 'folk society' or 'little community'. The temptation should be resisted. Both types are to be found everywhere. But it should be resisted principally because the notion of the face-to-face society is an inadequate means of describing multiplexity.

The idea that, in small-scale society, people interact with each other as 'whole persons' is a simplification. They may well encounter each other more frequently, more intensively and over a wider range of activities than is the case in more anonymous large-scale milieux. But this is not to say that people's knowledge of 'the person' overrides their perception of the distinctive activities (or 'roles') in which the person is engaged. It does mean, of course, that their knowledge of the person will inform their perception and evaluation of his or her activities, just as people's assumptions about their identities in the community will influence their strategy in role performance. Role and personality affect each other; there are no grounds for the generalization that one exercises an overwhelmingly deterministic influence over the other. Just as the stage actor strives for a convincing portrayal of his dramatic role — convincing in terms of *his* capacity to project a certain interpretation — so the social actor struggles to make his role performance congruent with his personality. Failure results in a performance unconvincing to others and/or to himself.

Attempting to identify those factors which led to men being judged as 'good' skippers in the Shetland island community of Whalsay, I found it impossible to generalize in a way which did not merely invite a host of exceptions. Whilst one could abstract a set of principles — for example, ideas of good seamanship, of successful man-management, of diligence, experience and canniness — it was clear that these were not applied uniformly within the community. Rather, the principles were interpreted and applied somewhat differently by and to different people, a flexibility of rule we shall meet again later in the context of an

Andalucian village (see Chapter 4, below). Moreover, skippers them-selves organized their own performance of their skipperhood in the light of their assumed public personae and of the history of their wider social relations with the members of their crews. For example, although a man is, in one context, skipper to his crew, he may also be their kins-man, or age-mate, or neighbour, or close friend from schooldays. How-ever, he has to make the crew regard him, in the wheelhouse, as skipper, rather than as cousin; otherwise he would be unable to exercise authority over them. But he cannot behave *qua* skipper in a manner which would be discordant with his customary and known demeanour in the com-munity. By the same token, it would be quite unacceptable for him to attempt to extend his authoritative position as skipper *beyond* the context of the fishing crew. Rather, his behaviour has to be that of cousin, friend or neighbour who happens also to be skipper (see Cohen, 1966).

Multiplexity thus calls for means of discriminating roles, not to de-personalize them, for they all merge in the person of the actor, but to signal to others appropriate behaviour. Gluckman observes that the characteristic means of demarcating roles is symbolic: 'The greater the multiplicity of undifferentiated and over-lapping roles, the more the ritual to separate them' (1962, p. 34), and that ritual 'operates to cloak the fundamental conflicts' which inhere in multiplexity (1962, p. 40).

We do not need to think of these ritual markers as having anything necessarily grandiose or ceremonial about them. Their symbolism, as we suggested earlier, may be much more mundane: perhaps residing in terminology, in mode of address, or in apparel. But, although it may be down-to-earth, its importance must not be underestimated, for the effective display of these symbolic markers provides much of the foundation of social order.

A vivid example of the dramatic use of symbolism in this regard is the comparison, given by Epstein, of the receptions accorded to two chiefs on the Zambian copperbelt (Epstein, 1978). The first, Chiti-mukulu, Paramount Chief of the Bemba, was largely unnoticed. People neglected to welcome him with the customary gestures of respect. At another venue, he was almost completely ignored. At a third, he was even physically abused. He was dressed as a European, and was travelling in a van. Epstein's informant comments that bystanders watching the chief's visit 'just looked at him as if he was an ordinary man' (1978, p. 31). Another, explaining his refusal to offer the chief a royal salute, said, '. . . look at this chief — the way he wears his shirt. And not even a tie' (p. 32). The second visiting chief, Mwata Kazembe, Senior Chief of the Lunda, was treated quite differently. He appeared resplendent in traditional dress, accompanied by musicians and dancers, generating tremendous excitement and enthusiasm. Explaining the difference, one man says,

> Many people turned up today because they heard that the chief had come with drums and dancers; had it not been so there would have been very few here. But that is what an important chief should do . . . He has to make people feel confidence and pride in him as an African chief. That is why your Bemba chief was not respected. (pp. 34–5)

A less colourful symbolic display, described by Carlen in her study of English magistrates' courts, uses space and language to delimit roles, with judgmental consequences, privileging some and putting others at a disadvantage. (Carlen, 1976). Similarly, Edelman (1964) notes how the Kafkaesque ecology of the bureaucratic labyrinth biases the interaction between bureaucrat and client, enhancing the power of the former, and handicapping the latter.

Examples like these can be found in profusion, vivid because they all describe the symbolic enhancement of behaviour, and demarcation of roles, on the public stage. But such public and political behaviour often shows up in dramatic form the commonplace behaviour of ordinary people in their day-to-day lives. So, when lecturer and students return to the lecture room from the bar where they have been enjoying a sociable lunch hour together, each has to be aware that their behaviour to the other must change accordingly. When a father ceases playing with his child and moves into 'disciplinary mode', he has, likewise, to signal the need for and to secure an appropriate change in the child's demeanour. In both cases symbolic devices (in the first, perhaps, of title, in the second, of tone) are deployed to mark the transition. In both of these cases, failure to distinguish adequately between the two postures would be as devastating as Chitimukulu's inability to command attention and respect.

In her brilliant account of Utku Inuit culture, Jean Briggs describes just such an unsuccessful attempt made by her adoptive father, Inuttiaq, the Utku's lay religious reader, to claim for himself authority which clearly impugned the equality of the band's members. The services which Inuttiaq conducted on Sundays and on other notable occasions in the Anglican calendar, were held in his iglu and were, therefore, extremely cramped, with 'twenty nine of us crushed into Inuttiaq's ten-foot iglu, contorted by the curving walls, by the uncomfortable proximity of foreign elbows and feet, and by the attempt to avoid the most relentless drips from the dome'. In deference to their surroundings, the congregation remained in the same posture throughout the service — until, one day, Innutiaq evidently decided that they should stand for the closing hymn. On the first occasion, they obeyed, despite difficulties. But within a very few weeks, tacit mutiny had broken out:

> The end came in February. For several services, Inuttiaq seemed to ignore the fact that the congregation remained seated; he made no sign that they should rise. The following Sunday he *whistled* the congregation up with an imperative jerk of his chin . . . but only (five) obeyed. He never ordered them up again; the status quo ante prevailed. (1970, pp. 55–6).

A further attempted innovation, in which he claimed clerical authority for his instruction that people should knock on the door before entering an iglu, proved similarly unsuccessful. We have to conclude that Innutiaq simply lacked the resources to mark out convincingly a new role for himself. Another classic study in which the diffuse strategies of such informal leadership are revealed is W. F. Whyte's celebrated *Street corner society* (1955). In this groundbreaking urban ethnography, Whyte describes social relations within and between gangs of 'corner boys', illustrates the skills deployed by the leaders — in bowling, courting, and diplomacy — to sustain their elevated positions, and demonstrates the consequences — loss of status and of the capacity to manipulate roles — when these skills lapse.

The apocryphal notion of the 'simplicity' of community, and the unqualified concept of the face-to-face society, are clearly inextricably related. As has been suggested above, and as I attempt to show throughout this book, social relations within the community may not be necessarily *more* complex than in other milieux. We ought perhaps to content ourselves by saying that they are different; but we cannot allow to pass unchallenged the view that they are simpler than those elsewhere. Similarly, we have to recognize that in all societies some relationships may tend more towards the personal, some more towards the impersonal. But to treat any relationship as being absolutely devoid of considerations either of role, or of person, would seem to be odd and certainly very partial. Certainly, in the small and close community personal knowledge and the primacy of the personality does not exclude a sensitivity to the boundaries of different activities, with their associated rights, obligations and sanctions. Thus, even to think of such a community as being *structurally* simpler is to be misled. As Simmel incomparably showed, the anatomy of social life at the micro-level is more intricate, and no less revealing, than among the grosser super-structures of the macro-level. This intricacy is itself an expression of the greater responsiveness of micro-society to the marvellously complicated individuals who people it; and it is that very responsiveness which, as we shall see, goes much of the way towards explaining the recent resurgence of community as a mobilizing idea in social action.

(ii) The myth of egalitarianism

A further corollary of the supposed simplicity of community life is a similarly apocryphal claim for its egalitarianism, again propagated by Redfield (e.g. 1955), but repeatedly perpetrated throughout the tradition of community studies which followed. The complaint we should make against this claim of egalitarianism is not that it is incorrect or empirically unwarranted, but that it is inadequate. It rarely distinguishes among equality as an ideology ('We should all be equal here'), as a rhetoric ('We are all equal here'), and as pragmatism ('We behave *as if* we were all equal here'). None of these should be confused with a description of actual social relations.

It is our contention that the unqualified attribution of egalitarianism to a community generally results from mistaking the absence of structures of differentiation — say, class, or formal hierarchies of power and authority — for the apparent absence of differentiation as such. The means by which people mark out and recognize status may often be concealed from the superficial ethnographer, masked as they often are, beneath protestations of equality and the paucity of institutional expressions of *in*equality. In part, the pragmatism of egalitarianism leads people to mute expressions of difference to which they are, nevertheless, sensitive. Thus, a community may lack formal structures of leadership. However, it will have means of attributing status and prestige, perhaps based on prowess in subsistence or other valued activities, or on age, or on evident sanctity, or whatever. For example, one observer convincingly calls into question the egalitarianism so commonly imputed to the fishing *outports* (settlements) of rural Newfoundland, the most easterly, and poorest, province of Canada:

> This writer's own experience . . . has been that all Newfoundland society is stratified, and that virtually all Newfoundlanders are critically aware of status differences. Moreover, we would argue that most rural communities are as highly stratified, if not more so, than the urban centres. The basis of this stratification is varied and may include religion, 'industriousness', work skills or a wide variety of other criteria. The status

symbols we have actually observed include the side of the
harbour one lives on; how often one paints one's house; the
amount of fishing gear one has; the quality of foodstuffs,
wild game, or alcoholic beverages one gives away; how quickly
after a snowstorm one shovels one's path or driveway; the size
of one's woodpile in summer when it is not necessary to have a
large one, and, in recent years, the acquisition of indoor
plumbing and furnace heating. Moreover, once an individual
or family gets assigned a status in rural Newfoundland it is
quite often impossible to escape or change it. Even sons take
on the supposed characteristics of father, and the process
assumes many of the qualities of self-fulfilling prophecy.
(Matthews, 1970, p. 224)

Status thus imputed may often be translated informally into influence
and authority. The important characteristic of this kind of differentiation is, though, that it is rarely publicly acknowledged: it is a tacit
recognition of difference. Indeed, one finds not infrequently that
some such communities may well have formal political structures —
councils and so forth — which speak officially for the community to
the outside world; but which have less credibility *within* the community than these more informally acknowledged 'leaders' (see, for
example, Frankenberg, 1957; Cohen, 1975). As we shall see later,
important, if tacit, gradations can even cut across the explicit and
dogmatic egalitarianism of some religious sects (see below, Chapter 2,
pp. 60ff).

So, every community generates multitudinous means of making
evaluative distinctions among its members, means of differentiating
among them which, although they may lurk beneath the structural
surface, are powerful components in local social life. Frequently, the
appearance of egalitarianism conceals the reality of differentiation (see
Hanrahan, 1979).

Ethnographers do not mistake apparent egalitarianism for its
reality just because they do not look hard or far enough. The mistake
has more complex roots which have to do with both pragmatic and
rhetorical expressions of egalitarianism. There are circumstances which
make it appropriate for people to behave as if they were equal. Imagine
the atmosphere of the cramped messroom in a trawler, in which men
live cheek by jowl week in and week out, year after year; if one or a
few claim superiority, or privilege, or rank over and above their formal
position in the crew it is a clear recipe for friction. Such potential
tensions have to be precluded, for there is no practical means of escape

from such fraught situations on the trawler at sea; people in such confined circumstances have to develop a reasonable *modus vivendi*, or
suffer the consequences (see the sensitive portraits in Warner, 1984).
The same may also be said of the rural, and fairly remote community
(as, indeed, of any rather isolated groups of people) in which a persis-
tent assertion by someone of his difference becomes an insufferable
irritant, and is not at all the same as the communal imputation of distinctive identity to individuals (see Cohen, 1978).

Isolation is not always a matter of geography or of special interest.
It may also be the product of seclusion behind communal boundaries,
such as those which communities contrive through symbolic means.
Here, pragmatic egalitarianism becomes also a rhetorical expression of
the integrity of the community. It is the presentation to the outside
world of the common interests of the members of the community. As
such, it bears the characteristic hallmark of communication between
different levels of society; namely, simplification. When a group of
people engages with some other, it has to simplify its message down to
a form and generality with which each of the members can identify
their personal interests. Otherwise the message becomes impossibly
convoluted and so heavily qualified as to be unintelligible to the outsider. Thus, when a position is stated 'on behalf of' a community — '*we*
want . . .' '*we* think . . .' — it implies a generality of view tantamount to
the expression of sameness, of equality. Dissent would impugn this
egalitarianism, just as it would offend the integrity of the boundaries
thus contrived. Such general statements of position, if not exactly
fictions, are often sufficient distortions of individuals' aspirations that
they would not pass *within* the community. However, the formulation
of such general positions for communication to another party often
also feeds back into the community to inform its sense of self, and
thereby embellish its symbolic boundaries.

Further, the expression of egalitarianism across the boundary may
often also be a means by which the community expresses its difference
from those elsewhere. Its members may denigrate the disparities of
wealth and power, or the competitiveness which they perceive elsewhere, to justify and give value to their espousal of equality. This,
also, is a way of giving vitality to the boundary.

Here again, then, we can see that egalitarianism, like personalism
in social relations, is a powerful symbolic aspect of social process in
the community, rather than an index of its structural poverty. In the
earlier theoretical renderings, egalitarianism was treated rather as a dull
sameness, and, in one notorious instance, as both a pathological expres-

sion *and* cause of a community's stultification and immiseration (Banfield, 1958). If we treat a community's putative egalitarianism instead as an item in its contrastive identity, rather than as a superficial depiction of its social structure, then we give ourselves interpretive access to the dynamic processes by which it symbolizes itself and its boundary.

(iii) The myth of inevitable conformity

Redfield argued that the less isolated a community became, that is, the more it came into contact with the metropolitan 'centres' of a society, the further it would travel along the continuum from the 'folk' to the 'urban' pole, with a consequent loss of the qualitative dimension of community life. Here we come to the very cores of two, related, contentions. The first displays an essential theoretical postulate of structural functionalism: that structure determines behaviour. The second is that, given this structural determinism, similar structural influences produce similar behavioural responses. We shall have a good deal to say about both of these contentions at various stages of this book. Let us just preface the argument by noting that, like the fallacies of the 'simple' society and of egalitarianism, it arises from an over-emphasis on the *form*, or appearance, and inadequate attention to, or neglect of the *substance* or meaning of behaviour.

The myth of inevitable conformity suggests that the outward spread of cultural influences from the centre will make communities on the periphery less like their former selves — indeed, will dissipate their distinctive cultures — and will turn them, instead, into small-scale versions of the centre itself. These culturally imperialistic influences will move outwards along the tracks of the mass media, of mass information, of spreading infrastructure, of mass production, national marketing and consumerism, ushering in a monolithic urban culture which will transform behaviour and will spell, what was called, 'The eclipse of community' (Stein, 1964). As we shall see later, the same kind of thesis was advanced for the transformation which would be wrought by 'modernization' and 'development' throughout the Third World. Both predictions have been discredited by history — except, perhaps, in the eyes of politicians — but were, in any case, anthropologically naive to the point of banality. They both assume that people can have their culture stripped away, leaving them quite void, then to be refilled by some imported superculture. They assume, in other words, that people are somehow passive in relation to culture: they receive it, transmit it, express it, but do not create it.

This view of culture was effectively undermined in sociology by the rise of social psychology, phenomenology and symbolic interactionism. British social anthropologists had been a little less gullible, certainly since first-hand ethnography began to accumulate with the development of modern fieldwork techniques. They noticed quickly that alien forms were not merely imported across cultural boundaries. In the act of importation, they were transformed by syncretism — by a process in which new and old were synthesized into an idiom more consonant with indigenous culture. But as anthropologists themselves began to recognize the multivocality of symbolism, and the problematic relationship between form and meaning, they also made it apparent that the transformation went beyond a mere marriage of idioms. Communities might import structural forms across their boundaries but, having done so, they often infuse them with their own meanings and use them to serve their own symbolic purposes. In Chapters 2 and 3 we shall see repeated examples of this process. Suffice it for now to note that, as a consequence, different societies, and different communities within the same society, may manifest apparently similar forms — whether these be in religion, kinship, work, politics, economy, recreation or whatever — but this is not to suggest that they have become culturally homogeneous. For these forms become new vehicles for the expression of indigenous meanings. Of particular interest to us is the irony that they may well become media for the reassertion and symbolic expression of the community's boundaries. These boundaries will be very difficult, if not impossible for the outsider to recognize. It is as if a cartographer used conventional figures in an unconventional way, without providing a key. The map becomes unreadable. Since community boundaries, now more symbolic, more 'mental' than physical and geographical, are unreadable, they are harder to breach. You cannot drive a bridge across a river which you cannot see.

The distance between centre and periphery, between the bounded community and the outside world, is now often of this conceptual variety. Indeed, the conceptual distance is elaborated and embellished to maintain the authentic distinctiveness of the community. Conformity is thus often an illusion; at the very least, it is only part of the story. The notion that communities will be transformed by the dominant structural logic of their host societies, rendering them more alike, ignores the indigenous creativity with which communities work on externally imposed change. Change in structural forms is matched by a symbolic recreation of the distinctive community through myth, ritual and a 'constructed' tradition. But, let us not anticipate the story too far.

CONCLUSION

I should not want to leave the impression that the work of the American masters can be blithely consigned to historical oblivion. It should be read, and not only for its historical interest. It was written with intellectual excitement, imagination and verve. It is full of insight; some of it, particularly Park and Burgess's observations on the management of information, has a strikingly modern ring to it, if not the enduring contemporaneity of Weber. But theoretically and methodologically, it has been left behind by the paradigm shifts in social science, and by the accumulation of ethnographic experience. But the wheel carries on turning, and their day may come again. However, it has been our contention that they did considerably muddy the waters in which the classical masters swam, and it is *their* heritage which bears most upon us. Students must read Durkheim, if they are to grasp contemporary approaches to symbolism and to oppositional modalities in social process; Simmel, for our concern with micro-social process; and Weber, to grapple with the problems of meaning and interpretation with which we are now so deeply (and, perhaps, neurotically) engaged.

It is precisely these latter problems that inform the approach taken here. Community studies were consigned for some time into an abyss of theoretical sterility by obsessive attempts to formulate precise analytic definitions (see, for example, Hillery, 1955). We are not concerned now with the positivistic niceties of analytic taxonomies. We confront an empirical phenomenon: people's attachment to community. We seek an understanding of it by trying to capture some sense of their *experience* and of the meanings they attach to community. Thus, moving away from the earlier emphasis our discipline placed on structure, we approach community as a phenomenon of culture: as one, therefore, which is meaningfully constructed by people through their symbolic prowess and resources.

2

Symbolizing the Boundary

INTRODUCTION

Comparative social science proceeds from the methodological assumption that the terms used to describe parts of one society may be properly applied to another. This assumption has provided a fundamental and irresolvable philosophical problem in social anthropology for it is tantamount to the view that one culture can be descriptively and, therefore, interpretively, reduced to terms which are appropriate to another. Protagonists of the method may claim that two or more cultures are sufficiently alike to be analysed through the use of common categories. Antagonists respond that their similarity is the contrived product of their subsumption under such common categories — that, therefore, the analyst merely renders them *as if* they really were alike. The philosophical problem is too complex to be pursued further here. However, we introduce it into our discussion because it bears crucially upon the substantive problem of community boundaries. Just as, in their attempts to understand and describe other cultures, anthropologists and sociologists trip over the concealed obstacles of cultural difference, so too do 'ordinary' people in their perception of and interaction with others. Anthropologists may reduce the extraordinary diversity among Trobriand matriliny, Tallensi patriliny and Choiseul Islands bilateralism to one of the descriptively simple categories, 'kinship' and 'descent'. But, in even more naive manner, lay people 'understand' other people's kinship or familihood by assimilating it to their own. That is, they place their *own* interpretive constructions upon other people's experiences and frequently confuse the two. Of course, we have to use our own experience as the starting point in our attempts to make sense of what we see around us. Indeed, when we are unable to do so, that is, when we are unable to thus translate the unknown into the knowable, we tend to become afraid. But this inclination to impose our meaning on the behaviour of others may provoke the other to insist upon the uniqueness, integrity or distinctiveness of his behaviour. In effect he or she says to us, 'but my experience is *not* like yours. My case is different!' Or, the ubiquitous adolescent outburst to all-knowing parents, 'You don't know me at all — I'm not the same as you!' It is much the same sentiment of distinctiveness that leads communities and ethnic groups to the reassertion and reaffirmation of their boundaries. Indeed, such assertiveness is likely to intensify as the *apparent* similarity between forms on each side of the boundary increases, or is imagined to increase. For the *appearance* of similarity may dissuade people from questioning its *reality*. Those who feel, in consequence, that their boundary has been blurred by the confusion, have then to expose the contradictions between appearance and reality. We will approach this aggressive assertion of distinctiveness as this chapter proceeds and, more squarely still, in the next chapter. First, we have to examine in greater depth the ways in which people become aware of their community's distinctiveness, the symbolic devices used to contrive and maintain this awareness, and, thus, the symbolization of community boundaries.

The various types of descent system mentioned above may all be amenable to the descriptive category 'kinship'. But we need to penetrate cognitively their own boundaries in order to gain any sense of how they are experienced and understood by their members. By the same token, to call both Buddhism and Anglicanism 'religion' does not give us any substantial basis from which to make sense of the experience of belief of any particular Buddhists or Anglicans. For that we need to find some more subtle and intimate access to their consciousness. When looking at other people's communities, therefore, we have to question the significance we might be inclined to attach to the appearance of their structural forms and seek, instead, the meanings imputed to them by their members. In other words, we have to treat them as *symbolic* forms.

Case: Gypsy and 'gorgio' perceptions of womanhood
A fascinating illustration of the differences of perception may be found

in Judith Okely's sensitive account of gypsy women. Writing on a general theme of the contrast between gorgio ('white') and gypsy views of gypsy women, she attributes to the white stereotype of the gypsy sensuality and sexual promiscuity. Against this, she shows gypsy women to be, in actuality, more concerned than their gorgio detractors with sexual propriety, fidelity and restriction. While the white community may see the gypsy as 'dirty', the gypsy has a more highly developed ideology of bodily purity and pollution than is generally current in British society. Indeed, the gypsies exploit their ideology to symbolize their ethnic boundary. Gypsies, says Okely,

> make a fundamental distinction between the inside of the body and the outside. The outer skin with its discarded scales, accumulated dirt, by-products such as hair, and waste such as faeces, are all potentially polluting. The outer body symbolizes the public self or role as presented to the gorgio. It is a protective covering for the inside, which must be kept pure and inviolate. The inner body symbolizes the secret, ethnic self. (Okely, 1975, p. 60)

Case: The Seychellois healer

Another eloquent illustration may be gleaned from an account of magical healing in the Seychelles. Here Marion Benedict, the white observer, much to the evident amusement of the healers (*bonhommes des bois*), initially approaches healing as if their clients naively believe in their magic. In other words, she succumbs to the imagery of magic in her *own* culture. She sees the healers' Seychellois clients as gullible; the healers as cynical exploiters of this gullibility. Only after long reflection and personal consultation with healers does she realize that the healers' art lies in the acquisition of information through gossip. Moreover, even their most avid clients are complicit in the provision of such information. Far from being gullible, they have some awareness of the therapeutic value of confidential talk. The ephemera of magic (*gris gris*) and the arcane paraphernalia of the *bonhomme de bois* may be no more than a means of masking the division between a stressful reality and the therapeutic fantasy of its successful negotiation; and, by the same token, a means of marking the boundary between the Seychellois and those who, in supposing them to be superstitious and gullible, reveal their own credulity — the whites (see Benedict and Benedict, 1982, especially pp. 92ff).

Anthropologists were long ago cautioned against confusing similarity of form with similarity of its substance. In the Introduction to his *Political systems of highland Burma,* Leach identifies the 'aesthetic frill', the ritual and symbolism with which societies embellish their routine and technical behaviour, as expressing the essence and, therefore, the distinctiveness of the society. Within these aesthetics lie the 'ethical rules' of society. This part of the content of an act may be materially irrelevant to the ostensible purpose of the act. But it is of crucial importance for the ways in which the participants map their social worlds: it is 'part of the total system of interpersonal communication within the group' (1954, p. 12). As such, although it may be unintelligible or even imperceptible to the outsider, it serves to express to the member the salience of his social boundaries. Although in the work cited above Leach was concerned with proposing an approach to the analysis of ritual rather than of social boundary, it will be evident that his insight into the symbolic element in routine behaviour is of the greatest importance to our topic. It emphasizes the argument, sketched above, that structural *form* must not be confused with *substance*: the meanings which people find in behaviour goes far beyond the functions or character of their behaviour as these may be perceived by others. Any behaviour, no matter how routine, may have a symbolic aspect if members of society wish to endow it with such significance (cf. Needham, 1979, p. 14).

Case: The Cyrenaican Bedouin

As an example, consider this description of tea drinking among Cyrenaican Bedouin, with attendant 'frills and decorations':

> During a session of tea-drinking, which lasts an hour or longer, numerous frills are added to the simple technique of boiling water, mixing it with tea and sugar, and drinking it. The proceedings begin with a brief argument about who is to make the tea. This decided, the little tea glasses and the small enamel tea pot are placed in front of him on a tray. Embers are brought in on a piece of metal and put near the tray. The water is boiled in a vessel called a *kilu* — a small can distributed by the Italians for holding the ration of a kilogram of oil during the days of the concentration camps. All these items are standard, and no others would serve the purpose. As soon as the tea-maker has put the water on to boil, the assembled men fall to conversing. They converse with conspicuous zest; not to do so would be improper. As the water comes to the

boil, the tea-maker pours some into the small teapot, adding a handful of tea and two or three handfuls of sugar. The conversation, meanwhile, continues unabated. After the mixture has been boiled to a thick syrup-like brew, the tea-maker fussily washes a few glasses, arranges them in front of him in a row, and then, from a great height, pours some tea into the little glasses, mixes it, and pours it back into the pot again. He then replaces the lid of the tea pot by slapping it shut with quite unnecessary vigour, as if angry with it. Three or four such mixings usually suffice. He then pours off a small amount of tea into a glass, again holding the pot extraordinarily high above it, tastes it, pours the remainder back into the pot, and, without comment, returns the pot to the smouldering embers, his every move watched with absorbed attention by those sitting around him. Depending on the general mood, the tea-maker performs these actions a greater or lesser number of times, before tea is finally poured into all the glasses and handed round. Each man brings the glass to his mouth in a circuitous trajectory, before quaffing the tea noisily. Three rounds of tea are offered by the camel-herding bedouin. Each round is prepared with the same flourishes. When the third round is complete, the men rise as if propelled and depart abruptly. (Peters, 1984, pp. 212–213.)

The author of this account insists that the routine he describes is not ritual, for 'tea-drinking does not alter the relationships of the people'. Yet, there is clearly very much more being done than the brewing and drinking of tea. The very conventionality or orthodoxy of each part of the procedure suggests that each is a statement of conformity to the body of norms established and recognized within given social boundaries. The tenor of Peters's description entitles us to suppose that a failure to observe these conventions would immediately mark the transgressor as outsider or as deviant. Peters notes that the participants view the procedure with 'absorbed attention' — hardly the attitude we might take to the mere boiling of a kettle. He notes a number of actions in the process ('flourishes') which are clearly materially redundant: the pouring of the tea 'from a great height'; the slamming shut of the teapot lid 'with quite unnecessary vigour'; the circular motion with which the drinker brings the glass to his mouth; and the noisy drinking. It is surely evident that, routine as this behaviour may be, to limit its description to the pragmatic business of ingesting tea would be to miss the point.

Peters's 'flourishes' are Leach's 'aesthetic frills'. Both identify the symbolic nature of such routine behaviour. There may be tea parties held in Boston and bedouin-land, but clearly their meanings for their respective participants is so very different that the descriptive label applied to them here serves only to obfuscate their character and significance.

THE BOUNDARY AND SOCIAL CHANGE

This issue of the confusion between form and substance, or between ostensible function and indigenous meaning, is important in the context of social change as communities become increasingly subject to influences from across their boundaries. The interrelated processes of industrialization and urbanization, the dominance of the cash economy and mass production, the centralization of markets, the spread of the mass media and of centrally disseminated information, and the growth of transportation infrastructure and increased mobility all undermine the bases of community boundaries. Each is a multi-pronged assault on social encapsulation, and one which results in an apparent homogenization of social forms. Within any country, the language, family structures, political and educational institutions, economic processes, and religious and recreational practices of communities come to have a certain apparent resemblance to each other. At the very least, they may seem to resemble each other more than they do those of communities in other countries. Such apparent similarity may well lead people to suppose that the old community boundaries have become somehow redundant and anachronistic. Indeed, the vested interests of the national media, national political parties, marketing specialists and so forth may well lead them actively to demean and denigrate sub-national boundaries. But this homogeneity may be merely superficial, a similarity only of surface, a veneer which masks real and significant differences at a deeper level. Indeed, the greater the pressure on communities to modify their structural forms to comply more with those elsewhere, the more are they inclined to reassert their boundaries *symbolically* by imbuing these modified forms with meaning and significance which belies their appearance. In other words, as the *structural* bases of boundary become blurred, so the symbolic bases are strengthened through 'flourishes and decorations', 'aesthetic frills' and so forth.

Much early development theory, of both capitalist and Leninist pedigrees, assumed that with 'development', the less 'modern' world would come to resemble the modern in respects other than just the economy. Law, kinship, politics and religion would all tend towards a societal norm (see Worsley, 1984, especially pp. 1–22.) Indeed, as we know, such assumptions provided much of the ideological charter for European and American imperialism. We know also that the application of such assumptions by colonial governments, missionaries and other, shadier, figures produced a ubiquitous phenomenon of resistance cloaked in atavistic, nativist ideologies and rhetorics, of which the cargo cult, *négritude,* 'African socialism', and the southern African Zionist churches have been celebrated examples. We have been less sensitive to similar, if less explicit and dramatic, kinds of reaction from bounded groups and communities within our own national boundaries – partly, perhaps, because, although they are expressions of determined difference, they are masked by an *apparently* similar structural form; and appearances, as they say, are deceptive. This reaction may be manifest in a variety of aggressive political statements of the community's integrity, perhaps stressing language rights, emphasizing special problems or claiming certain amenities. This politicized assertion of boundary has its less solemn aspects too, as for example in an impassioned debate conducted through the correspondence columns of the *Shetland Times* in 1978 following objections by the Shetland Women's Group – a body then composed entirely of outsiders – to the plans of a local club-owner to bring a striptease artiste to perform in Shetland, for the entertainment principally of the oil-related construction workers then present in large numbers in the islands. The idea of striptease in the inclement north was widely regarded locally as laughable, but what was clearly seen as the patronizing intervention of outsiders was not so regarded. Two of the campaigners wrote:

> Recently my friend and I were involved in the Shetland Women's Group campaign against the striptease show . . . We were shocked by the undeniably rascist reaction of many Shetlanders whom we approached to sign our petition. 'Get back home! Who asked you to come here?' The objection of many was not to the issue but rather to what they saw as our misplaced involvement in Shetland matters. (18th August, 1978)

To which came the reply:

> I am not at all sure why they call themselves the Shetland Women's Group, while admitting they are *soothmoothers* (outsiders). Furthermore, whatever gave them the idea that Shetland womanhood was about to be exploited, and that they were qualified to prevent such an unlikely event taking place? (25th August, 1978)

And, again,

> Isn't it rather significant that none of the five letters (protesting against the strip-show) was written by a Shetlander? What would happen to me if I went to their countries and started shouting the odds . . . in the name of the local people? (8th September, 1978)

This aggressive commitment to a bounded community also takes less explicit forms. It may be discerned in the ways in which people use, regard and revise some of their customary social forms and practices. It has long been noticed that societies undergoing rapid, and, therefore, de-stabilizing processes of change often generate atavistically some apparently traditional forms, but impart to them meaning and implication appropriate to contemporary circumstances. Such reactions to change may be a syncretistic marriage of tradition and modernity in language, technology, religion and so forth. They are also sometimes manifest as a deliberate maintenance of the forms of customary practices in changed circumstances which now render their earlier rationales anachronistic. These syncretic techniques appear to be means of rendering alien practices into a familiar and, therefore, acceptable form. They may be regarded as vernacular translations and modifications of extrinsic social influence. However, this view of the influence of the 'outside world' on a bounded community is over-simple. It is a digestive model of social change in which the body (the bounded community) is seen as being essentially transformed by the ingestion of food (extrinsic influence) which it absorbs through the action of its own digestive juices. However, social change is often marked also by a regurgitative process which is more than mere flatulence, but amounts to a veiled refusal to swallow! The social analogue of this chewing of the cud is the adoption by a community of the structural forms originating from outside which are transformed in the process of importation and fundamentally reconstituted with indigenous meaning, In this way structures imported across the boundary provide new media for the expression of native values.

Case: The Naskapi

The Naskapi Indians are based on Davis Inlet on the coast of Labrador, but spend much of the year hunting in the interior hinterland known as the Barrens. Since 1952 their contact with the outside world, largely in the forms of the Hudson's Bay Company and of the Newfoundland and Canadian Governments, has been mediated through the resident Catholic missionary. He has introduced to them new fishing technology, helped them to acquire houses at Davis Inlet in place of their tents, has nurtured their desire for material goods and, therefore, their need for cash. According to their ethnographer, the missionary's strategy has been to make the Naskapi increasingly dependent upon the settlement at Davis Inlet in order to bind them more closely to the mission located there (Henriksen, 1973, p. 15).

One of the most important symbolic expressions of Naskapi communality is the commensal ritual of *mokoshan,* the sharing and eating of Caribou bone marrow. Like sacrifice in some pastoral societies, mokoshan may be held to mark any significant transformation in social relations, but also to signify the authority of the *wotshimao* − the temporary leader of the hunt − or to celebrate successful hunting. Mokoshan is customarily regarded as 'a confirmation of the relationship between the hunters and the Caribou Spirit' (Henriksen, 1973, p. 10) and is a ritual with its roots deep in the Naskapi's shamanistic past. It would therefore seem to be anathema to the proselytizing interests of the Catholic priest.

Mokoshan is essentially a ritual of the hunting grounds − the Naskapi's world − and, therefore, is seldom warranted in the settlement of Davis Inlet itself − the interface, or boundary, with the White's world. There, the rituals of the Church appear to prevail. But do they really do so?

> Holy Communion, which is by far the most important church ritual for the Naskapi, is very similar to *mokoshan*. In fact, the Naskapi say that Holy Communion is the same as *mokoshan*. This is a reasonable equation, as a comparison between the two rituals shows that they consist of similar elements: both take place within one tent/house, one man being chief of the ritual; in both, there is a small amount of sacred food that must be handled and eaten with the utmost care: in *mokoshan,* it is the raw marrow of caribou bones that is the vehicle of communication with the Caribou Spirit, while the bread and wine unite the communicants with the body of Jesus Christ in Holy Communion. (Henriksen, 1973, p. 78).

And so while Father Pieter feeds his flock with the body (but not the blood! (*ibid.*)) of Christ, and gives thanks for the conversion of the pagan, the Naskapi chew on the wafer and commune with the Caribou Spirit. In so doing they contemplate the essence of Naskapi culture and reaffirm their community's boundaries.

A rather similar instance has been reported concerning another eastern Canadian Indian group, the Micmac of Nova Scotia. Once again we find a very clear demonstration of the ways in which the members of a community can take an alien social form, and fundamentally transform it symbolically so that it refracts their own sense of collective self and shores up their communal boundaries against their subversion from outside. One example is the Micmac's reformulation of a Catholic saint's day:

> at the time of first European settlement, the chiefs gathered on the coast in summer to carry out political deliberations. At the same time, the family bands gathered together to celebrate their common bonds, renew alliance, arrange for marriages, and so on. In due time, the Jesuits managed to insert some Christian content into the feast, and before long, the summer gathering became a feast of thanksgiving to St Anne, the new patron saint of the Micmac. Today, St Anne's Day is still the most important tribal event of the year, but not primarily as an occasion to renew the covenant with the protector saint, but rather as an instrument of ethnic incorporation, an occasion to communicate Indian unity and claim to nationhood. (Larsen, 1983, p. 47)

Case: The Permai funeral

Like *mokoshan* among the Naskapi, a commensal ritual, the *slametan*, provided an important symbolic expression of communality in Javanese village life. Part of its social effectiveness lay in its common recognition as a medium of neighbourliness both by Moslems and Hindus. Indeed, it exemplified the syncretist solution to religious pluralism which enabled the adherents of different religions to live in social harmony. In the town of Modjokuto, as elsewhere in Java, this consensus became increasingly threatened by the rise of the Santri movement, a fundamentalist Islamic tendency. At the same time the old syncretic *Abangan* tendency was underpinned by the emergence of Marxism and of secular nationalism, and found political expression in the Permai party. The apparently syncretic character of Permai is evident in the following description:

> Permai meetings follow both the slametan pattern, complete with incense and symbolic food (but without Islamic chants), and modern parliamentary procedure; Permai pamphlets contain calendrical and numerological divinatory systems and mystical teachings as well as analyses of class conflict; and Permai speeches are concerned with elaborating both religious

and political concepts. In Modjokuto, Permai is also a curing cult, with its own special medical practices and spells, a secret password, and cabalistic interpretations of passages in the leaders' social and political meetings. (Geertz, 1975b, p. 151)

However, its apparent evocation of the customary syncretism of the slametan and so forth is belied by its character as an anti-Islamic party. Hence, Geertz's passing remark about the exclusion of Islamic chants from the ritual. The party also campaigned for secular burial, a practical impossibility in Modjokuto because of the long history of Islamic influence on the funeral ceremonies, and because the Modins, local religious leaders traditionally responsible for the conduct of funerals, were instructed in 1954 not to participate in the funerals of Permai members.

The ensuing difficulty is manifest in the case of a Permai member's frustrated and unsuccessful attempts to organize the burial of his young nephew who had been staying with him at the time of his sudden death. The Modin refused to cooperate and the entire funeral process, usually enacted within hours of death, was stalled, causing extraordinary emotional displays and fears of mystical calamity. It was only when the dead boy's father arrived, requesting a 'completely Islamic' funeral that matters could proceed, and the burial be carried out in the prescribed, Islamic, manner. Javanese funerary rites were customarily restrained affairs, and organized around a series of commemorative slametans. However, the first slametan held three days after the boy's death departed abruptly from the traditional form, with the Permai officials using the occasion to indulge in a long political discourse.

From Geertz's account, it is evident that the new sensitivity to social boundaries — in this case, of politico-religious groups — is finding expression in the very ritual form which, in the past, had masked and muted divisions. Whilst both sides recognized the legitimacy and force-fulness of the slametan *form* for the ritual marking of death (Geertz, 1975b, p. 164), each is now also using it as a medium for the expression of its own distinctly sectarian identities. The ritual, consensual and syncretic in form now communicates an ethic oppositional and novel in character and substance. Particularly striking is the fact that the funeral slametan is taken across the boundary, and — heavily coloured by Islamic influence — is used as a platform for anti-Islamic Permai doctrine. As one of Geertz's informants told him ruefully, 'you can't even die any more but what it becomes a political problem' (Geertz, 1975b, p. 156).

RITUAL AND THE BOUNDARY

All of these examples show that, whatever may be the apparent functional character of a structure, its substance may be largely constituted by its symbolization of the community's boundaries. The symbolic expression and affirmation of boundary heightens people's awareness of and sensitivity to their community. This phenomenon is well-known to political activists who often justify their apparently fruitless or hopeless demonstrations by pointing to the effect they have of 'raising consciousness' among participants. Indeed, this kind of rationale may well explain attempts by totalitarian regimes to find a political dimension in *all* aspects of political behaviour, whether in art or petty theft, a tendency described by David Apter as 'political religion' (Apter, 1963).

People participate in rituals for all sorts of reasons. But, whatever their motivations or ostensible purposes, it would seem that much ritual also has this capacity to heighten consciousness. It should not be surprising, therefore, to find ritual occupying a prominent place in the repertoire of symbolic devices through which community boundaries are affirmed and reinforced. In the remainder of this chapter, we shall review examples of some of the different ways in which ritual and cognate symbolic processes appear to be particularly efficacious in this regard.

(i) Rituals and the experience of communality

In his magisterial sociology of religion, Durkheim argued powerfully that religion and ritual provided both context and medium for the affirmation of a society's fundamental principles of organization. As both theory and ethnography have since proliferated, anthropologists have come to see ritual as very much more complex, and as having a far greater range of competences than Durkheim envisaged. Not the least important development was Malinowski's recognition of the psychological effectiveness of ritual. Although ritual, as a topic, brings out all the paradigmatic diversity and sectarianism of anthropology as a discipline, most exponents would agree that both in its social and psychological consequences, ritual confirms and strengthens social identity and people's sense of social location: it is an important means through which people experience community.

Our thesis has been that the symbolic expression of community and its boundaries increases in importance as the actual geo-social boundaries of the community are undermined, blurred or otherwise weakened. Evidence to substantiate this thesis may be found not only in settled communities, but also among those whose members have been dispersed and for whom ritual provides occasions to reconstitute the community.

Case: The peyote hunt of the Huichol Indians

The Huichol Indians of the Sierra Madre Occidental in north-central Mexico live in considerable isolation and poverty. The population, estimated to be between 4,000 and 5,000 are dispersed among five settlements in an extensive and mountainous area. Another 5,000 have spread throughout Mexico. The Sierra Madre Occidental Huichol communities are acephalous. They are not linked to each other organizationally, and are described as resembling 'a cluster of bands more than a true tribal organization' (Myerhoff, 1974, p. 62). Such integration as they have is provided only through 'a sense of commonality'. This sense appears to be most powerfully stimulated by the series of rituals which constitute the 'hunt' for peyote, which involve the Huichol in a pilgrimage to Wirikuta, the land of their divine ancestors and, therefore, of their origins. The juxtaposition of this sacred territory with their present, mundane homeland embraces a complex set of oppositions which express a fundamental contradiction. In Wirikuta, the Huichol are divine, trans-social, immortal and timeless. They experience a total fusion of man and nature and a perfect unity among all the elements of life. The boundaries which, in the mundane world, divide people and separate them from nature and the gods, are ecstatically diffused. Wirikuta is paradise (Myerhoff, 1974, pp. 258–61). By contrast, in the mundane world the Huichol is imprisoned by the 'social matrix' and dominated by the constraints of nature and ecology in

> a way of life which necessitates ceaseless, monotonous, and often ill-rewarded attention to the crops, the seasons, and accommodation to an ill-understood, ever-threatening pressure exerted by surrounding powerful and dangerous outsiders.
> (p. 259)

In their ritual return to Wirikuta the Huichol thus 'find their life' – their true essence – symbolically expressed in the deer ('the past life of perfection'), the maize ('the mundane, human dimension'), and the peyote ('the spiritual, private and free part of life') (p. 262) – which is denied to them in their contemporary, impoverished and sedentary conditions.

The boundaries between these two opposed states are marked symbolically in a number of ways. On the pilgrimage, the *hikuritámete* (pilgrims) assume the identities of the gods. To do so they engage in elaborate reversals. For example,

> One addressed someone in front of him by turning to the rear
> and one accepted something from another by telling him,
> 'You are welcome', so that the giver replied, 'Thank you'.

'Everything', says their leader, the *mara'akame*, 'should be upside down
and backward' (p. 149). They go through a series of purifications,
washing away and burning their corruption. They even refrain from or
conceal or transform the normal bodily functions both of ingestion and
digestion:

> Wirikuta is utterly pure; defecation is impure there because
> it is a conspicuously mortal activity and brings to the sacred
> land the other realm — home, everyday life, 'reality' — which
> has no place there . . . So too, boundaries between Wirikuta
> and everyday life are observed when the *hikuritámete* return
> to the home fire all bits of food they have consumed in the
> sacred land.

Food eaten in Wirikuta must not 'be contaminated by being trans-
ported into the other realm, the world of everyday life, (p. 242, n. 3).

Symbolism thus constitutes the boundary between the mundane
and sacred lives of Huichol. The *mara'akame* insists that the symbolism
is not translatable — in the sense that it is not a fanciful or allegorical
expression of belief and ideal. Rather, it is treated by the Huichol
literally. However, it seems reasonable to suppose that the euphoria
and 'collective ecstasy' (p. 157) which the pilgrims experience in Wirikuta owe much to the contrast between Wirikuta and their everyday
circumstances. Prominent among these is the marginality of the Huichol
to *mestizo* Mexico, a Mexico they have to cross on their journey to
the sacred homelands. The symbolic boundaries they create therefore
mark off not only their mythical past from their empirical present.
They also divide their community from the surrounding society — all
the more effectively because the symbolism is unintelligible to the
mestizos. In a wonderfully vivid description, Myerhoff recounts the
visit of the pilgrims to a rather smart restaurant on their journey
home from Wirikuta. Trooping past 'a crew of very elegant, haughty
waiters', the pilgrims, in their spectacular but now soiled pilgrimage
costumes throw food around 'in a sacred hail', rendering the menu and
accoutrements into a fantastic mythology, and delighting in the fact
that the poor *gringos* see only a party of outrageous and 'filthy Indians'
and cannot perceive their 'invisible treasure',

> realizing that no outsider could tell that we had been trans-
> formed, knowing that others only saw us as mortals. (pp.
> 167–8)

This statement powerfully evokes the efficacy of symbolism in boundary maintenance: it creates a sense of belonging, of identity – and, by the same token, of difference from others. It does so in ways which may well be unperceived by these others and which, hence, cannot easily be attacked or subverted by them. The symbolic process of the peyote hunt can be said to create a communality even among a group of people for whom the *structures* of community have been severely diminished and, perhaps, stigmatized. Huichol rituals clearly create a consciousness of community.

(ii) Rituals as symbolic markers

To the outsider Huichol symbolism is arcane, mystifying and, without very deliberate and specialized intellectual effort, impenetrable, to the extent that the outsider would be unable to recognize much of it *as* symbolism. For example, we might look with aesthetic admiration at a Huichol yarn-painting, and yet be quite unaware that the deer in the corner of the picture condenses a compendium of highly significant meaning for the Huichol.

But in many societies boundary-marking rituals are less esoteric and are frequently more explicit in expression. They may be large-scale and elaborate entertainments like Carnival, diffuse and festive occasions such as fairs and fiestas, or more focused local and parochial affairs, such as saint's days and shrine-specific celebrations (for example, in England, the Derbyshire well-dressings). In rural societies, and before the spread of capital-intensive technology, the agricultural cycle generated a ritual calendar, both religious and secular. But more 'modern' industrialized and secular societies also reveal important calendrical rituals marking locality, ethnicity, occupation, or some other significant aspect of communal identity. It is worth noting that even in those societies which have officially disparaged religiously oriented ritual, the state has found it expedient to contrive occasions for ritual performance (see, for example, Humphrey, 1983; Binns, 1979, 1980). Though these ritual forms are more explicit, it does not follow that their meanings are necessarily fixed and uniform. Rather, the ritual occasions are themselves symbolic. They have an 'official' form and rationale, but their participants may well find in them quite different meaning and experience. Indeed, it is probably the very opportunity they afford to their participants to assimilate the symbolic forms to their individual and idiosyncratic experience and social and emotional needs that makes them so compelling and attractive.

These rituals communicate on a variety of levels. In V. W. Turner's terms, they are 'multi-referential' and 'multi-vocal' (e.g. Turner, 1967,

1969). At the level of group-as-a-whole, of orthodoxy, they say something about the relation of the group to others. At the level of individual participant, they speak of the individual's relation to his group and to the world as mediated by his group membership. Both construct and allow the individual to experience social boundary.

Case: The Notting Hill carnival

The Notting Hill carnival is the largest and best-known West Indian celebration held annually in Britain. An analysis of its history since its formation in the mid-1960s suggests that it has passed through three quite distinct phases, all of which have been significant markers and celebrations of social boundaries and group identity. During the first, between 1965 and 1970, Carnival is described as, '. . . an expression as well as an instrument of . . . class solidarity' (Abner Cohen, 1980, p. 68). Notting Hill was a largely working class area which contrasted starkly with the then prevalent image of London as 'swinging' and affluent. Indigenous British and West Indian residents joined together in various struggles for local amenities, and Carnival expressed and stimulated the solidary local consciousness.

The second phase (1971—75) was more emphatically ethnic and atavistic, reaching back into the Trinidadian tradition of carnival which the black, newly emancipated but still colonized population took over from their white settler masters. Carnival was later developed and modernized in Trinidad as an emblem of Independence. The historical process of subjugation, assertion and eventual triumph was symbolized in the indigenous creation of the steel 'pan', whose combination in bands was to provide the symbolic essence of Carnival in Trinidad and, later, in London. The ethnic dimension to London's carnival was sharpened by the burgeoning of racial tension and the increasingly disadvantaged status of blacks in a period of growing unemployment. The carnival and its steel drums epitomized the confrontation with white Britain:

> with its rust, rough edges and clumsy appearance, the pan is a symbol of poverty and social disadvantage, a protest that in lands of plenty, endowed with so many sophisticated musical instruments, a people should be forced to pick up abandoned shells to express their artistic feelings. (Abner Cohen, 1980, p. 71).

The carnival was expressive; but also, says Cohen, fostered the spirit and substance of communality among its participants.

In the third phase (1976—79), the carnival was again transformed, reflecting in its composition the new elements − the young, assertive, Rastafarian-oriented youth of Jamaican origin − comprising the ethnic mosaic. This development was apparent in the confrontation of very different styles (for example, the live steel band, as opposed to recorded reggae), and in the emergence of black feminism as a significant feature in Carnival organization.

But throughout these different phases and transformations, Carnival is,

> an expression of and an instrument for the development of a new homogeneous West Indian culture, transcending islands of origin affiliations, in confrontation with the economic and political realities for the West Indians in contemporary Britain. (p. 78)

The salient boundaries and symbols of the participating groups change together, each stimulating and articulating the other. It is clear from Cohen's account that Carnival was symbolically effective at the micro-level also. He describes individuals − mask-makers, designers, musicians, organizers, band followers − who found a sense of ethnic identity for themselves through their activity in Carnival. Where previously as young immigrants they had felt rootless and unable to identify either with their society of origin or of settlement, they now found psycho-social orientation within the boundaries marked by Carnival. Each is able to define the community for himself using the shared symbolic forms proffered by the carnival.

Here, then, we return to the characteristics of symbolism outlined in the first chapter: it is the very ambiguity of symbols which makes them so effective as boundary markers of community. Victor Turner, one of the most influential anthropologists of symbolism, argued that some rituals − in particular, some ritual pilgrimages − have the capacity to create *communitas*, an identification among members which is so absolute as to be tantamount to the stripping away of all those social impedimenta which would otherwise divide and distinguish them. However, the efficacy of symbolism which we have seen described in this chapter, indicates precisely the opposite: that people can participate within the 'same' ritual yet find quite different meanings for it. It is precisely this assimilability of symbolic form to individual need which led another anthropologist, Michael Sallnow, to dispute Turner's attribution of *communitas* to pilgrimage. Writing about pilgrimage in the Peruvian Andes, he argues that the component symbolic forms − icons, rituals and so forth −

> *sacralised the boundaries and discontinuities between the different groups of devotees . . .* Indeed, it would be more appropriate in such circumstances to see community, not *communitas*, as the hallmark of pilgrimage. (Sallnow, 1981, p. 177) (my italics)

A similar boundary-marking competence is evident in the description of another local celebration, 'the Glorious Twelfth'.

Case: The Glorious Twelfth in Kilbroney

The twelfth of July is one of the major festivals in Protestant Northern Ireland, ostensibly recalling the Battle of the Boyne, but now explicitly celebrating oppositional Protestantism, the Crown and the union with Britain. Its modern connotations are eloquently expressed in the banner slogans paraded in the small town of Kilbroney:

> 'Fear God – Honour the King'; 'If God Be For Us – Who Can Be Against Us?' 'For the Throne is Established By Righteousness'. (Larsen, 1982b, p. 280)

The Protestants in the town prepare the celebration for weeks, painting their houses, hanging bunting across the streets, buying new clothes for the children. On the day itself, the parade, preceded by pipe bands, ends in a service, a succession of political speeches thinly veiled as religious sermons, and is followed by family picnics, games and music.

Larsen argues that Kilbroney, like other towns in Northern Ireland, is a composite which includes two quite separate communities, the Protestant and the Catholic. This dualism is reflected in all local institutions except the politico-administrative since, she says, Catholics do not have access to political office. It is also territorial, since the working class elements of the two groups live in *de facto* segregated areas. Further, it is underpinned by conventions of behaviour which maintain this separation and which Larsen refers to as rules of mutual 'avoidance'. But these boundaries also have various symbolic means of expression, ranging from the decoration and visual appearance of their premises (Larsen, 1982a, p. 132) to festivals, celebrations and rituals such as the Glorious Twelfth.

Larsen suggests that the symbolic efficacy of the Twelfth is clearly divisible into two categories: as a message from the Protestant community as a whole, which is mediated through its 'official' spokesmen in the Orange Order; and as a medium through which the 'ordinary' participants can discern and communicate those values in which they perceive their identity. In this latter regard, Larsen describes it as 'a demonstration of individual statuses within a 'macro' frame of social categories' (1982b, p. 285). Here, the sense of Protestantism as an oppositional category does not invoke history or theology but, instead, 'cleanliness, order, responsible management of property' (*ibid.*), all values denied by Protestants to Catholics:

> 'One-third of this population', [says a speaker at the rally], 'doesn't speak the same language as we do'.

The multi-vocality of the celebration permits participants to thus communicate with each other about themselves and, simultaneously, to communicate in various ways with different outside audiences. For example, in expressing *their* commitment both to the 'true faith' and to the Crown, they also distance themselves from the mainland British who are regarded as wanting, or even delinquent, in these matters:

> The symbol of this attitude is the Ulster flag, prominently displayed, its fresh colours contrasting with the faded union jacks that have served for so many years. (1982b, p. 287)

As a predominantly working-class celebration, they also distance themselves from their more middle class co-religionists who may be somewhat discomfited by the explicit display of sectarianism. But, at the same time, the ambivalence of the ritual symbolism is also exploited to suggest an egalitarianism evident in participation in the march by political and industrial leaders. It is apparent that the variety of values attributable to the Twelfth is so broad that the celebration acts as a compass by the use of which the lay members of the Protestant working class can orient their varying and idiosyncratic social identities:

> Participation in the celebration of 'the Twelfth' is not a status activated once a year, then discarded until next July. The event involves total social persons, who for a period of weeks and months are called upon to display their important qualities as responsible managers of property, affectionate parents, good neighbours, devoted Christians and respectable citizens. (1982b, p. 290)

The commemoration of the Glorious Twelfth thus exemplifies the multivalence of community and its boundaries. It symbolises the character of the community as a whole *vis-à-vis* groups 'on the other side' of the boundary. Further, it provides the constituent members of the community with the acceptable terms of reference in which to formulate, express and evaluate personal identities. The 'community', in this regard, is a cluster of symbolic and ideological map references with which the individual is socially oriented.

(iii) Symbolic reversal

The most striking feature of the symbolic construction of the community and its boundaries is its oppositional character. The boundaries are *relational* rather than absolute; that is, they mark the community *in relation to* other communities. It has been suggested that *all* social identities, collective and individual, are constituted in this way, 'to play the vis-à-vis' (Boon, 1982). Indeed, it has been argued that the very nature of symbolism itself contains not merely the competence of discrimination, but the sense of negation: in other words, that the very rationale of symbols is that they are different in some way from the entities they symbolize (Babcock, 1978).

We must now add a further dimension of complexity to this subject in order to examine another ubiquitous phenomenon of symbolism in community life, in which people not only mark a boundary between their community and others, but also reverse or invert the norms of behaviour and values which 'normally' mark their own boundaries. In these rituals of reversal, people behave quite deliberately and collectively in ways which they supposedly abhor or which are usually proscribed.

These symbolic uses of reversed or inverted convention have been noted throughout the world, although in widely varying forms. One of the most celebrated such descriptions concerns the Naven rites of the Iatmul tribe in New Guinea. These are occasions of explicit gender and generational reversal; and of the negation of customary circumspection in sexual display and comportment. Naven rites mark occasions, and particularly first occasions, when a person accomplishes a task which, though standard, is valued in the culture. Such tasks may range from homicide to building a canoe and catching fish. The rituals are thus, simultaneously, both a celebration of the individual, the *laua,* by those who stand in a certain relationship to him or her and, also, a celebration of the community itself since it is accomplishment in its valued behaviour which triggers the ritual.

The reversal noted here would seem to be quite different in significance from those observed by the Huichol in Wirikuta. There the pilgrims are concerned to emphasize the duality of their lives and the absolute differences between their mundane existence and their life in Paradise. But Naven appears to do precisely the opposite: it celebrates the normal, the 'standard cultural act' (Bateson, 1958 (1936), p. 6).

Another classic anthropological instance of reversed normality are the events described by Gluckman as 'rituals of rebellion', examples of which were the Zulu women's ritual worship of *Nom Kukulwana,* and the Swazi *incwala* ceremony (Gluckman, 1963). Like Naven, these involve reversals of normal gender behaviour and convention. but more-over, they take the form of a protest against established authority:

> women have to assert licence and dominance as against their formal subordination to men, princes have to behave to the king as if they covet the throne, and subjects openly state their resentment of authority. (Gluckman, 1963, p. 112)

Gluckman argues that these ritualized rebellions, associated with sig-nificant moments in the agricultural cycle, actually preserve, and defend the political systems within which they occur. The enactment of con-flict, 'emphasises the social cohesion within which the conflicts exist' (p. 127). The *incwala* ritual celebrates the endurance and permanency of the kingship as opposed to the transience and imperfection of the king. 'Every rebellion therefore is a fight in defence of royalty and kingship . . .' (p. 130).

The rituals, says Gluckman, ease tension. Moreover, their very institutionalization and codification is testimony to the capacity of established order to contain and defuse disorder.

Gluckman's analysis has been criticized both on grounds of theory and of his ethnographic interpretation. However, these criticisms do not question his assertion that these rituals are symbolic, if stylized reversals of apparent normality. One of his more recent critics suggests that they be seen as 'rituals "against" rebellion':

> the sacred dispraises of the Ncwala prevent rebellion by strengthening the loyalties between a king and his public where they are most likely to break down. (Apter, 1983, p. 530)

What is at issue here is more the definition of the salient 'normality' rather than the functions and efficacy of the symbolic devices them-selves. Clearly, the performance of the rituals points implicitly to the prevailing social order and 'marks' it in contradistinction to others.

Following the pioneering work of Bateson and Gluckman, rituals of reversal have been documented in many different cultures and, of course, the anthropological theories which follow in the wake of such ethnographic observation have proliferated. The inversion of the norm is not limited to ritual, but may be found also in all manner of symbolic forms. For example, an increasingly common response to the imposi-tion of stigmatic identity appears to be an assertion by those stigmatized of the characteristics which 'spoil' their identity (see Goffman, 1963), rather than to mask them. In a famous study of confrontations between Saami (Lapps) and 'white' Norwegians, Harald Eidheim shows how Saami in public contexts employ a variety of ruses to mute or conceal their Lappishness, and to assimilate themselves to the Norwegian-ness of a particular milieu. It is only in the privacy of their own homes, or in milieux where only Saami are present, that they fully assert their ethnicity, in language, humour, food, song, and general deprecation of the host society (Eidheim, 1969). However, a more recent strategy observed among ethnic and other disadvantaged groups has been to 'honour' the stigma, to render it as a positive value, and, thereby, to destigmatize it. Perhaps the most powerful and innovative use of this tactic lay in the assertion by black militants in the United States in the late 1960s, that 'Black is beautiful!' The impact of this message was all the greater for its contrast with the more defensive rhetorics which had previously prevailed in the politics of civil rights and race relations. The earlier claim had been for equality; the new one was a statement of superiority, and thus constituted a reversal of the 'normally' perceived scheme of things.

The same kind of ideological and rhetorical transformation has marked the politics of the women's movement during the last twenty years. While initially the struggle was for 'equal opportunity', for 'liberation' from the constraints of sexual prejudice and disadvantage, it later changed into a much more militant and seemingly chauvinistic assertion of the virtues of an exclusive feminism. These kinds of tactical and symbolic reversals have swept away the orthodoxies of relations between the powerful and the disadvantaged. In the areas of ethnic and 'centre–periphery' relations they have generated what one writer has called 'symbolic competition' in which the apparently disadvantaged group rejects the symbolic code in which it *is* disadvantaged, and replaces it by its own in which it is relatively powerful or to which it has exclusive access (Schwimmer, 1972). These 'opposition ideologies' (Schwimmer, 1972, p. 120) assert '. . . the superiority of the minority, although by worldly standards it may be categorized as an oppressed and exploited minority'.

Schwimmer treats such symbolic competition as a kind of surrogate for the worldly competition in which the minority is too handicapped to have any chance of success. This use of alternative symbolism is often to be found among religious sects whose membership is relatively underprivileged.

Case: The Focaltown Pentecostalists

The community of Focaltown, in central Newfoundland, was undergoing a period of rapid growth and modernization and was experiencing the full impact of materialism and consumerism during the late 1960s (see Cohen, 1975). The days had now passed when the population depended upon a monopoly employer for logging work in the woods, and upon the same person, in his other guise as merchant, for the supply of consumer goods through the redemption of his wage tokens. Three copper mines were being worked locally; other firms competed for lumber; and the old mercantile monopoly had been broken by aggressive entrepreneurialism. The earlier form of commercial relationship, built upon credit and 'truck', had been replaced by cash, partly through transfer welfare payments from the Canadian government, and partly through the employment market. The situation was thus marked by a burgeoning middle class bringing all the materialistic pressures of North American life into the Newfoundland *outports* (rural communities) for the first time.

Set against this picture of growth and prosperity was an unemployment rate among the able-bodied male population of 19–23%. Unemployment was so endemic in the rural Newfoundland economy that redundancy frequently meant long-term, and even permanent unemployment (see Wadel, 1973). To be unemployed in Focaltown during the late 1960s was to be doubly disadvantaged. One was not merely 'on the dole', but also thereby excluded from the novel accessibility of luxury goods and, therefore, deprived of the ability to compete in the new status game of conspicuous consumption.

Many of these long-term unemployed turned to the Pentecostal Assembly which, with 42% of Focaltown's population among its congregation in 1969, was then the largest of the several Protestant denominations in the community. Although unemployment was so rife throughout Newfoundland it still carried a stigma, especially in the self-consciously modern and innovative Focaltown. It is reasonable to suppose that Pentecostalism, although heavily tainted in the Province by this stigma, offered a means of coping with it. The Pentecostalists conducted themselves as a closed community. They operated their own schools, proscribed participation in religiously mixed social events, excluded themselves from most of the town's many voluntary associations, and concentrated themselves within a discrete residential section. They patronized only certain shopkeepers, and offered their political allegiance to only one of the community's competing factions. It thus became:

> a community with closed boundaries in which one may seek security and obscurity in the company of people who have shared the same worldly experience of negligible opportunity, poverty, and a limited knowledge of the social environment. It is a society into which people may withdraw having felt

> misplaced or displaced in the secular world. (Cohen, 1975, p. 103)

The defensive and protective effects of the sect's closed boundaries was further enhanced by the practice of public confession, providing the member with the opportunity to absolve himself of any guilt he may have felt about his worldly situation. The assertion of the boundary clearly produced a bond of solidarity among the membership.

But the Pentecostalists did not merely segregate themselves from the hostile world. They also created a new system of symbolic status in which they alone could participate, and which denied the validity and legitimacy of the symbolic arenas from which they regarded themselves as excluded. Pentecostalism

> is a religion in which the experiences of the present world are made bearable by being made trivial: this life is simply a preparation for one much more important — and sweet — which will follow.

It offers to the member,

> an escape from the competitive status-seeking of the material-istic culture in which he is isolated and frustrated by his poverty. 'Secular' status is rhetorically denigrated within the Assembly. Rather, status is ascribed on the basis of 'religious' criteria as manifest, for example, in one's virtuosity at speaking in tongues. As Wilson points out (1967, p. 154), 'Pentecosta-lists never weary of debunking worldly social status and of emphasising the unequalled significance of election by the Holy Ghost as the only status which really matters.' (Cohen, 1975, p. 103)

It is important to note that Pentecostalism was a highly assertive — indeed aggressive denomination. Its members publicized their activi-ties widely, denounced outsiders, and loudly deprecated those beyond its boundaries. In this respect, it 'advertises' the stigma with which its members feel themselves to be branded. Indeed, it wields the stigma almost as a challenge to others. It uses the stigma as a symbolic means of asserting and embellishing its own boundaries — indeed, as a means of constructing an alternative community.

In different societies and at different historical periods the symbol-ism of religion has been frequently and powerfully deployed to challenge the superiority of a dominant politico-symbolic system. Rastafarianism, first in Jamaica and now among 'emigré' populations of Jamaican descent, heresy in medieval France (Le Roy Ladurie, 1980), even Mau

Mau in colonial Kenya, are all examples of such 'opposition ideologies' and competing symbolisms which contrive community.

SYMBOLIC REVERSALS AND SELF-AWARENESS

In the preceding section we have seen instances of the use of a symbolic reversal of normality first to emphasize and reassert the norm; and, secondly, to reject it and to assert another in its place. The first is concerned with ensuring the continuity of community; the second is oriented more to the very creation of community. Both operate by constituting social boundaries symbolically.

In the final section of this chapter we encounter in some detail a use of symbolic reversal in which both of these earlier varieties are combined. People create a symbolic world which is a kind of fantastic reconstruction of empirical society: the dialectical contrast between the two is resolved by a reassertion of the inevitability and desirability of the first through recognition of the fantasy and impossibility of the second. Through such symbolic behaviour, people draw the conventions of community about them, like a cloak around the shoulders, to protect them from the elements − *other* people's ways of doing things, other cultures, other communities. The conventions become boundary through their re-investment with symbolic value.

Case: The Balinese cockfight

A brilliant exposition of such a reversal is contained in Clifford Geertz's account of cockfighting in the Indonesian island of Bali (1975c). Geertz's analysis directs us to see the cockfight as a metaphorical commentary on the nature of Balinese village society. However, before relating it to its wider social context, let us first look at the cockfight as an event which is understandable and explicable in its own terms. This is not to suggest that it is adequately or properly understandable in its own terms, merely, that they do provide a certain sense of the event.

Cockfighting was an illegal but widely practised activity in Balinese villages, with matches often held on public holidays. They are occasions also for betting − and the significance of this gambling is central to Geertz's explanation. Matches are made only immediately prior to the fight, with an owner seeking 'a logical opponent' (1975c, p. 421) for his cock. Part of the logic lies in matching birds as evenly as possible, in order that the outcome of the fight should be maximally unpredictable. It is clear, also, that this logic extends to the search for social eveness as well.

The cocks fight with five-inch long razor-sharp swords attached to their legs. The attaching of these spurs is a highly specialized task with which only a few local men are entrusted. The spurs themselves are protected by astronomical and gender taboos and are treated as ritual objects. The fight is divided into rounds, marked by the time it takes to sink a pierced coconut in a pail of water. The intervals between the rounds are also timed by a sequence of coconut sinks, and provide the opportunity for the cock's handler to nurse the wounds received in the previous round and to try, by all manner of means, to stimulate the cock to victory:

> He blows in its mouth, putting the whole chicken head in his own mouth and sucking and blowing, fluffs it, stuffs its wounds with various sorts of medicines, and generally tries anything he can think of to arouse the last ounce of spirit which may be hidden somewhere within it. . . . Some of them can virtually make the dead walk . . . . (1975c, p. 423).

Often both birds will be mortally wounded, but always the rule is that the bird which expires first loses the fight. Geertz paints superb contrasts between the violence and tumult of the fight, and the absorbed, but *silent* attention of the spectators. Moreover, he juxtaposes the 'wing-beating, head-thrusting, leg-kicking explosion of animal fury' (p. 422) with 'a vast body of extraordinarily elaborate and precisely detailed rules' (p. 423) recorded in palm-leaf manuscripts and bequeathed from generation to generation as an integral element of locally esteemed lore and tradition. At the fight, the guardian of these codes is the umpire, whose authority is absolute and unquestioned. Thus, the fight, furious, bloody, and defined by the state as unlawful, nevertheless is conducted and perceived by the villagers as in accordance with 'the civic certainty of the law'.

Geertz characterizes these contrasts in a way which recalls fundamental postulates of Lévi-Straussian structuralism as one between nature — 'rage untrammeled' — and culture — 'form perfected'. However, as we shall see, the structure of the fight does not celebrate only 'culture' but, rather, 'cultures' — or, at least, a culture's sense of itself *vis-à-vis* others.

So, one way of looking at this event is to treat it simply as a match between two fighting cocks — as a sporting entertainment — in much the same way that we might watch a football game. A cockfight is a cockfight and, at the same time, a demonstration of a society's rule-making prowess. But the matter is clearly not so simple as this. Geertz suggests that the fight is only superficially between the cocks. A more comprehensive view would be to see it as a fight between their owners. Significantly, the word 'cock' has the same double meaning for the Balinese as it has in colloquial English, adding point to this interpretation of the cockfight: men fight each other with their cocks. The double meaning clearly suggests an identity between the man and his bird, although for the Balinese the bird symbolizes a man's *social* self rather than his sexuality. The distinction is important.

Underlying this association between the man and his cockbird is an intriguing reversal of the Balinese norm regarding the symbolic value of animals. Generally, an animal is polluting, the more so the closer it is to the ground. By this scheme of things, the cock should be a serious pollutant. People normally avoid animals: they avoid touching them and even avoid speaking about them. Animals are filth. But the fighting cock has an extraordinarily cossetted and privileged existence. It is pampered and perfumed, groomed, specially fed and watered, extravagantly housed and sheltered, doted upon and frequently handled and exercised. It would seem, then, that the cock is not regarded as belonging to the animal world at all. Although the Balinese do not impute human characteristics to it, their exceptional view of the cock does indicate that they regard it as a kind of extension of its owner. In a sense, it is himself, and it is in this sense that Geertz refers to the fighting cock as an 'ambulant penis'.

The cockfight, then, is a metaphorical contest between men. If we look a little further at the event itself we shall be able to see further evidence for this view. Ostensibly, the cockfight is a match between two birds. More substantially, it is a contest between their owners. But there is another activity going on as well, for the contest is not only expressed in 'inter-cock' violence but in a contest between men whose ostensible form is money — 'ostensible' because, as becomes clear, this currency or form is more apparent than it is real. The cockfight is, as noted above, the occasion for extensive betting. This betting is of two kinds. The first, and key bet Geertz calls the 'centre' bet, and it is made between the two owners. It is always an even money wager. Here, part of the logic mentioned earlier becomes salient. The more evenly matched the birds, the higher is the bet. Another way of putting this is to say that the more unpredictable the outcome, the greater is the cost of losing.

Through the betting we can also relate the cockfight and its principles to the wider fabric of society. For the centre bet also influences the nature of the betting which is going on among the spectators. While the centre bet is always for even money, the outside betting is always for odds. The higher the centre bet the more unpredictable is the outcome, and therefore the greater is the tendency for the side betting to be on short odds. Like the fight itself, the side betting is a scene of apparent chaos and clamour which is actually informed by a highly orderly, well-understood and codified process. The bets are made through a gradual focusing of matching shouts among the throng, the odds-taker (backing the 'underdog' cock) shouting the short-side *number* of the odds he wants; while the odds-giver (backing the favourite) replies by screaming not a number but the *colour* of the cock in question. Again, the sense of significant contrast:

> As the moment for the release of the cocks by the handlers approaches, the screaming, at least in a match where the centre bet is large, reaches almost frenzied proportions. . . In a large-bet, well-made match – the kind of match the Balinese regard as 'real cockfighting' – the mob scene quality, the sense that sheer chaos is about to break loose, with all those waving, shouting, pushing, clambering men is quite strong, an effect which is only heightened by the intense stillness that falls with instant suddeness, rather as if someone had turned off the current, when the slit gong sounds, the cocks are put down, and the battle begins. (pp. 428–9)

In the connection between the centre bet and the side betting there is expressed a direct link between the individual and the collectivity which makes the cockfight an inherently *social* event. This is substantiated by another element too. We have seen that the ideal is for the centre bet to be large – the larger the better – for this means an increased likelihood that the cocks will be evenly matched. It means also that the contestants have more to lose. Indeed, the wagers become, what Geertz calls, a 'deep play', a game in which the costs of losing are so great that it may be economically irrational for the contestants to engage in it at all. But the centre bet is not merely between the owners. The money for the bet may be put up by a number of people. The backers are always the owner's close social associates – kinsmen, members of his descent group, close friends, near neighbours and so on. The contest, then, far from being merely between individual owners, is better seen as one between social factions. Moreover, the factionalism informs the side betting as well as the key centre bets, for side betting observes a number of rules which are evocative of the conventions of segmentary affiliation which Evans-Pritchard imputed to the Nuer. For example, a man never bets against a cock owned by a member of his own kin group. 'Usually he will feel obliged to bet for it, the more so the closer the kin tie and the deeper the fight' (p. 437). Betting, then, is less a wager than an affirmation of alliance. Another rule is that if a man's own kin group is not involved he bets on the bird belonging to the kin group with which his is more closely associated. By the same token, if a cock from his village is matched against one from another village, he would back the 'home' bird. Two cocks from the same social group are rarely matched against each other. People from opposed social groups will bet very heavily against each other. The cockfight now appears as a sociological index of the village.

What is at stake in the cockfight? It could hardly be the prestige of owning the 'best' bird since we know that animals generally are negatively valued and that, therefore, we can only understand the positive value vested in the cocks by treating them as 'non-birds' – as symbols of human, and social beings. Money? Well, although the money may not be insignificant the concept of 'deep play' suggests that it is token rather than object.

Geertz argues that victory in the contest affords the victor the opportunity to impugn the prestige and honour – the appurtenances of social status – of the vanquished. Status cannot actually be contested for it is not mutable. Rather, the cockfight is a dramaturgical account of what life might be like if status *could* be the subject of competition. Bali is a Hindu society and, as such, is rigidly stratified on ascriptive bases. So, if born low, a victorious cockfight does not afford a man the opportunity to climb the status ladder; if born high, an ignominious defeat in the ring would not mean descent of the status snake. But fleetingly, momentarily, it exposes human vulnerability, the flesh and blood beneath the rigid social structure of a caste system. Of course, there are none who fall so hard as the high born and, because of the ideological premium placed on the high centre bet (the 'social' component of the logic of an even match) cockfighting is largely an affair between the higher status citizens. Moreover, as we have seen, the cockfighting contestants are also social opponents, being drawn from opposed factions or groupings. This circumstance also makes victory particularly sweet and defeat particularly galling. Status cannot be changed by the outcome of the fight, but a point has been made and scored:

> All you can do is enjoy and savor, or suffer and withstand, the concocted sensation of drastic and momentary movement along an aesthetic semblance of that (status) ladder, a kind of behind-the-mirror status jump which has the look of mobility without its actuality. (p. 443)

The cockfight, then, is a metaphorical commentary on the social life of the Balinese village. It is a sense of their society which the Balinese themselves make (p. 440). Geertz puts it this way:

> It provides a metasocial commentary upon the whole matter of assorting human beings into fixed hierarchical ranks and then organizing the major part of collective existence around that assortment. Its function . . . is interpretive: it is a Balinese reading of Balinese experience, a story they tell themselves about themselves (p. 448).

The cockfight is a fantasy, a picture of what Balinese society might be like if it was not trammelled by the rigidities of status, the constraints of convention and of tightly controlled behaviour. This fantastic reversal is a kind of speculative and harmless experiment in social change which does not actually cause change nor weaken the social order. It has the effect of highlighting precisely those mechanisms which *do* trammel behaviour, which *do* constrain people, and which *do* organize them in their customary ways. It is, therefore, a symbolic exposition of the distinctive characteristics and qualities of Balinese social organization and culture, a textual lesson in what it means to be Balinese. As Geertz says,

> Attending cockfights and participating in them is, for the Balinese, a kind of sentimental education. (p. 449).

In considering Geertz's case study one is repeatedly struck by the fact that the events and behaviour it describes are, in almost every particular, a reversal of the Balinese norm. Cocks are adored, whereas 'normally', animals are loathed and loathsome. Passions are expressed, whereas they are normally strictly controlled. Status is put on the line whereas in normal circumstances it is recognized as immutable. Ostensible disorder is generated whereas normally the very highest value is placed upon the maintenance of orderly behaviour. These reversals are dramatic ways of expressing the norms — and, thereby, of being able to value them. Elsewhere I have described a similarly dramatic reversal of normality — though, in this case, one which has not been repeated — in a study of an organized fishermen's protest in Shetland (see Cohen, 1982a).

The protest took the form of a blockade of the principal harbour in the Shetland Islands in 1975, during which nearly all of the fishing crews in the Shetland fleet struck and combined themselves and their boats into a single entity under the command of an elected officer to disrupt the normal operation of the harbour. Like the cockfight, this too reversed normality in many respects. The Shetland men from the community I study (the most important fishing community in Shetland) almost never engage in public in any assertive behaviour, let alone in an organised demonstration. They do not believe in the efficacy of such action and, indeed, would disagree about its ethical and pragmatic justification. 'Normally' they would inconvenience themselves rather than inconvenience others. Normally they would rather have faced almost any eventuality rather than abandon their independence by combining with others. Yet, there they were, submitting themselves to the authority of one of their own number as commander. Normally they would regard as stupid and/or wasteful any fisherman who willingly spurned the opportunity to go to sea to fish — yet, there they were, sitting in harbour for four days and nights when they might otherwise have been at sea filling their holds. Normally they would proscribe any action which risked damage to their boats or danger to their crews. Yet, in the blockade, they risked both.

This is not the occasion to reiterate the analytic reconciliation of these apparent contradictions. Suffice it to say that engaging in behaviour which departed so radically from the norm served to make the fishermen dramatically aware of the norm, so that it could again be celebrated, broadcast, re-asserted against its subversion, and, therefore, be maintained.

We began this discussion with the axiom that people become aware of their culture when they stand at its boundaries: when they encounter other cultures, or when they become aware of other ways of doing things, or merely of contradictions to their own culture. The norm is the boundary: its reversal, a symbolic means of recognizing and stating it. Such awareness is a necessary precondition for the valuing of culture and community. The process of evaluation is accomplished through the use of symbolic devices such as those we have discussed here and is a pre-condition for its maintenance. It rests upon the contrivance of symbolic boundaries.

3

Communities of Meaning

INTRODUCTION

As we saw earlier, much of the attention previously paid to the community by social anthropologists and sociologists concentrated upon the structures and forms of community organization and life. By contrast, the argument has been advanced here that such a focus tends to make unjustified assumptions about the meanings which structural elements have for the members of communities and, therefore, mistakes their significance. We have been attempting to re-focus the analysis on meaning, rather than on form, and in order to do so we have taken *culture*, rather than structure, as our point of departure. Further, we have suggested that since people become most sensitive to their own culture when they encounter others', the apposite place at which to find their attitudes to their culture (or their imputation of meaning to their community) is at its boundaries. We have found that as the structural bases of the boundary become undermined or weakened as a consequence of social change, so people resort increasingly to symbolic behaviour to reconstitute the boundary; and we have looked at examples of such symbolic behaviour.

Having thus suggested that symbolism does have this efficacy and competence, we must now turn to the difficult questions of 'how' and 'why'. Part of the answer to the first question has already been touched on in the earlier suggestion that symbolism does not so much carry meaning as allow people to impute meaning to it. Hence, the argument of Chapter 1 that the 'same' symbol can 'mean' different things to different people, even though they may be closely associated with each other as members of the same community or bearers of the same culture. The same is true also of 'community' in its role as symbol.

COMMUNITY: STRUCTURE OR SYMBOL?

When, in the past, communities were described as morphologies, as composites of social structure, the issue of meaning did not arise. Sociologists argued that the elements they described were objectively apparent, their objectivity warranted by the use of 'scientific method'. In Durkheim's terms they were 'social facts'. If it was objected that the meaning of these social facts was different for the sociologist than for the members of the community he described, the response was that the sociologist was objective; the members were not. The Marxist version of this riposte was to declare the dissenting view 'falsely conscious'. Stated in such abbreviated form these perspectives appear decidedly arrogant. However, they were borne out of rather more profound intellectual convictions. These writers took the view that structure determines behaviour. If, for example, one designates a particular structure as 'classroom', one is thereby legislating about what will happen there. It will be used for teaching; it will be a milieu in which, for most of the time, one person will speak and many will listen. Should it transpire that it is used for different purposes the judgement would be made that normality had been suspended, either through the imposition of another structural form (for example, the classroom used as a bar for the P.T.A. dance) or through the pathological breakdown of structural order (the pupils riot).

When Durkheim laid such heavy emphasis on the necessity for adequate structural integration to forestall *anomie*, he intended precisely such a consensus of meaning, a compliance with structure. By the same token, Marx saw the imposition of 'forms of consciousness' as the means by which the State contrives compliance with the prevailing order, be it the dictatorship of capitalism or of the proletariat.

These perspectives provided the dominant traditions of thought and analysis in social anthropology and sociology well into the second half of this century. They logically enjoined the propriety of describing communities in terms of their constituent institutions, classes and sectional interests. Since structure was supposed to determine behaviour, it would follow that people similarly located in the social structure would behave in similar ways — such behaviour including perception and meaning. It was therefore assumed that one could describe communities and their constituent parts in terms of uniformities or orthodoxies of meaning: 'Italians do "x"'; 'trades unionists think "y"'; 'the elite say "z"'. Indeed, as we noted in Chapter 1, there had long been established a taxonomy of communities, again with a Durkheimian impress, based essentially on a crude counting of structural components: those which contained only a few differentiating elements were labelled 'simple'; those with a relatively greater number were 'complex'. It would follow that the members of 'simple' societies would tend to think alike; whereas the members of the different structural parts of a 'complex' society would think differently from each other, coinciding only with their structural peers. If, therefore, one wanted to know how people thought, it was necessary only to examine the structure.

$$\text{structure} \longrightarrow \text{meaning}$$

If there was room for symbolism at all in this perspective, it was only as a means of expressing some identifiable meaning. 'Symbols', it was said, 'stand for something else' — but the relationship between the symbol and the something else for which it stood was not in doubt.

$$\text{structure} \longrightarrow \text{symbol} \longrightarrow$$

The dominance of these theories of structural determinism was broken in due course by the complementary influences of Weberian sociology and Mead-ian social psychology, influences which fractured sociology into many contending factions such as those of 'interpretivism', phenomenology, ethnomethodology, interactionism and so forth. Social anthropology was fortunately able to withstand such fragmentation, but its agenda was effectively changed: 'meaning' was recognized as problematic, and the expression of meaning — symbolism — became as prominent a focus for study and analysis as structure had been previously. When once students of anthropology had had to be drilled in the algebra of kinship analysis, they were now immersed in the philosophical complexities of belief and knowledge.

These developments were very much more complicated than a mere recognition of the cognitive distance between the observer and the observed — a distance often somewhat misleadingly portrayed as a confrontation between so-called 'etic' and 'emic' approaches. The very recognition of this distance logically calls into question the observer's (etic) assumption that there may be *an* emic view, rather than views. If we impute a religious belief to the Nuer — say, their conceptualization of the divinity, *Kwoth* (see Evans-Pritchard, 1956) — we are excluding the possibility or probability that their religious beliefs are as ill-defined, various, fuzzy and inarticulate as our own. Put it another way: we should not regard a person's description of himself as Anglican or Catholic as an adequate description of his beliefs. Such a description is one of affiliation, not of philosophy. Any two Catholics may say to each other, 'I believe in God', and, because they share the vocabulary imagine that they 'understand' each other. Such an assumption would often be unjustified: the words 'God' and 'believe' may mean rather different things to each of them. Similarly, they may share the same symbolic forms for the expression of belief — the Mass, genuflection, wearing a crucifix — and yet each be expressing quite different things. A society masks the differentiation within itself by using or imposing a common set of symbols. Previous generations of anthropologists and sociologists saw their task as the description and analysis of this public medium. But modern ethnography has to discriminate between the common mask and the complex variations which it conceals.

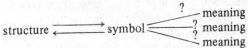

The problem is not reserved to the academic social scientist. Indeed, it was our belated recognition of it as a *universal* problem of social interaction which gave it its new status in the study of social behaviour. As members of society we are all continuously engaged in the struggle to understand other people's behaviour. What passes as *understanding* is often based on *interpretation,* and the interpretation is generally accomplished by reconstructing other people's behaviour as if it was our own: in other words, by attempting to put ourselves in their shoes, our minds in their bodies. Hence, when other people use words which we use, we *interpret* their intended meaning by assuming that it corresponds to ours. Sometimes it may; sometimes it may not; but even in those cases where it does not we may be quite unaware of the discrepancy — as in the case of the congregation of co-religionists all, apparently, doing and believing the 'same' thing. We are all, then, engaged continuously in interpretation. The anthropologist, as student of social behaviour, is just faced with one further level of difficulty in seeking to offer, in Geertz's phrase (1975a), an 'interpretation of others' intepretations'.

The earlier sociological orientation to structure was, essentially, an orientation to the common mask. Our emphasis upon culture focuses upon the diversity beneath the mask. It seeks interpretations, and the means by which they are made, rather than objective form. 'Community' can no longer be adequately described in terms of institutions and components, for now we recognize it as symbol to which its various adherents impute their own meanings. They can all use the word, all express their co-membership of the 'same' community, yet all assimilate it to the idiosyncrasies of their own experiences and personalities.

The so-called 'simple' society, like Durkheim's mechanical solidarity, is thus revealed again as a gross sociological simplification. The community boundary is *not* drawn at the point where differentiation occurs. Rather, it incorporates and encloses difference and, as Durkheim asserted for his organic model, is thereby strengthened. The boundary represents the mask presented by the community to the outside world; it is the community's public face. But the conceptualization and symbolization of the boundary from within is much more complex. To put this another way, the boundary as the community's public face is symbolically simple; but, as the object of internal discourse it is symbolically complex. Thus, we can all attribute gross stereotypical features to whole groups: but, for the members of those groups such stereotypes applied to themselves as individuals would almost invariably be regarded as gross distortions, superficial, unfair, ridiculous. Such stereotypes provide material for the comedian and for tabloid journalism; they are our caricatures of other people. But they have no validity as accounts of how people see themselves. In the public face, internal variety disappears or coalesces into a simple statement. In its private mode, differentiation, variety and complexity proliferate.

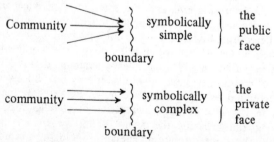

The boundary thus symbolizes the community to its members in two quite different ways: it is the sense they have of its perception by people on the other side — the public face and 'typical' mode — and it is *their* sense of the community as refracted through all the complexities of their lives and experience — the private face and idiosyncratic mode.

It is the private, idiosyncratic mode with which we are primarily concerned, for it is here that we encounter people thinking about and symbolizing their community. It is in these depths of 'thinking', rather than in the surface appearance of 'doing' that culture is to be sought.

SYMBOLISM AND SOCIAL CHANGE

It is precisely this distinction between the superficiality of structural form and the profundity of its conceptualization which validates the argument that structures imported into a community do not necessarily undermine the community's boundary nor blur its distinctiveness. For, since structure determines neither behaviour nor attitude it follows that members of different communities may use similar structures, yet think about them in quite different ways. Indeed, as we saw in the cases of the Naskapi and Micmac Indians, people can turn these alien structural influences to the service of their indigenous symbolic systems and thereby symbolically reinforce their customary boundaries.

Cultures, ways of thinking, attachments to community, are much more resilient than many scholars of society have supposed. Marx, at least, recognized that the socialist revolution would require the full panoply of state power in order to transform people's ways of thinking. Later writers, particularly Americans of the structural–functionalist persuasion, saw much greater malleability in behaviour. For example, the once-prominent psychologist David McClelland, proposed, in all seriousness, that the underdevelopment of the Third World might be substantially alleviated by imbuing subsistence peasants with the motivation to be 'achievement-oriented' capitalist entrepreneurs (McClelland, 1966). They required intensive treatment with 'N-ach', the achievement factor, and they would then replace their subsistence livelihoods with market-oriented production, a doctrine not far removed from some of the more simple-minded elements of Conservative philosophy in this country. This kind of thinking went beyond economics to constitutional law and public administration as well. Thus, the British colonial authority everywhere sought to leave replicas of its own governmental, judicial and administrative institutions behind when it vacated Government House in favour of the Independence government, supposing, with well-intentioned arrogance, that the superiority of these structures over the indigenous forms thay had replaced would turn the previously colonized peoples into models of their own civic selves. These structures would generate an ideological commitment to Anglo-American versions of democracy, which two further American political scientists dignified as the 'civic culture' (Almond and Verba, 1963).

The disproof of these arguments is obviously due to their naiveté, rather than to the perversity of Indian peasants and African politicians. They are arguments which, in assuming the manipulability and shallowness of culture, failed to recognize the creativity of societies — indeed, failed to understand culture at all. Even if African parliaments did adopt some of the procedure and ceremonial of the British parliamentary system, they were not 'doing Westminster in blackface', but were exploiting a medium of alien origin for the conceptualization and expression of essentially indigenous ideas. As Thomas Hodgkin succinctly observed, ideologies cannot be exported in the same way as bicycles (1964, p. 60). In the very process of importation they are transformed.

The moral to be drawn from this rather wordy discussion is that in looking for the distinctiveness of communities — that is, in seeking their boundaries — we should not be deceived by their *apparent* similarities into supposing that they are *actually* alike, nor even that they are becoming less different. The residents of Wandsworth, Winnipeg and the Western Isles may all spend much time watching the television — indeed, watching the same television programmes — may use the same terminology to address their parents, may affiliate to the same religious denominations, may observe the same calendar and the same life-cycle ceremonies, and may apparently be dominated by the same economic imperatives. But none of these apparent convergences of life-style entitles us to suppose that the cultural boundaries which separate them are now redundant and anachronistic. As we saw earlier, it became fashionable during the 1960s for Western sociologists to talk about the 'eclipse' or 'end' of community, arguing that the spread of the mass media, the growth of centralized state power and the seemingly inexorable tendency to urbanization had eradicated meaningful distinctions within societies except those marked by economic status and, in particular, by relations to the capital market. In other words, community had given way to class. Later, others were to argue that class itself had been superseded, and that the salient categories were those of gender, race, and whether or not one was employed. Clearly, all such contentions are axiomatic: they are neither provable nor refutable, but depend upon the metaphysics of definition.

By contrast, it is empirically undeniable that the 1970s and 1980s have seen in the Western world a massive upsurge in sub-national militancies founded on ethnic and local communities. The aggressive assertion of locality and ethnicity *against* the homogenizing logic of the national and international political economies has marked the renaissance of community. This is not surprising: it is this logic which attacks the old *structural* bases of community boundaries. Communities therefore respond by rebuilding their boundaries on symbolic foundations.

Case: The Norwegian Saami and the Alta River protest

During the last three or four hundred years the arechtypal economic life of the Saami or Lapps of the interior of Finnmark in northern Norway was one of nomadic reindeer pastoralism. Even now, with many Saami living settled lives with sedentary occupations, one hundred thousand animals are moved over a migratory route of two hundred kilometres by two hundred herding families. The timing and route of the migration is dictated by a combination of biological factors and ecological strategy. Thus, for example,

> the annual spring migration reflects (*inter alia*) the animals' need for protein (grasses) and pastoralists' wish to save the rich lichen beds on the tundra for the winter. This kind of intermeshing of the needs of herd and herder is the first prerequisite of reindeer pastoralism. (Paine, 1982, p. 11)

Once the herders have imposed a migratory timetable upon the herd, they become bound by it, and change is difficult and risky. Herding also involves complex collaborative arrangements among different households in cooperative units known as *sii'da*. Reindeer pastoralism thus clearly calls forth social as well as ecologic strategies which ultimately produce the pastoral 'circuits' (Paine, 1982, p. 13).

The success of the circuit is fraught with hazard and uncertainty. The weather can obscure the location of animals; some reindeer wander off, whilst deer from other herds may intrude. The successful reproduction of the herd demands skilful herd management, to reduce the stress to which animals may be subject during the autumn rutting season, and to try to ensure optimal conditions for the spring calving. In such extreme climatic conditions as those of the tundra, this kind of husbandry can be disrupted by the slightest alterations in the migratory route of the circuit.

It was a more than slight disruption that was presaged in the plans by the Norwegian government to develop a hydroelectric project on the Alta River. In the report cited above, Robert Paine catalogues in detail the potentially damaging effects which the construction of the dam might have on the reindeer of the Nuortabealli sii'da. The picture he paints of the annual migratory cycle focuses upon the extreme sensitivity of herded reindeer, the tenuous ecological niches in which they are pastured and moved, and the skill and fine judgement demanded of the Saami in herd management. He presents evidence from other similar developments to show that hydro construction exacerbates the first two elements, and brings the third to nought (for example, p. 31). The area in which the Alta project was planned has been used successfully by Saami in their reindeer pastoralism since the seventeenth century for their spring and autumn camps. Its topography, says Paine,

> is an ideal one for working with reindeer. The unbroken tradition of use of the area by Saami is, then, no accident. (p. 34)

Indeed, its importance has increased due to the loss of traditional pastures elsewhere. The actual site of the project is the area where herds are pastured while awaiting their turn to move south to the winter pastures. It provides a crucial 'marshalling' pasture in which the various migrating herds can be kept properly separated and fed and in which they find appropriate conditions for the rut. It is, therefore, of immense strategic importance. Paine concludes,

> the serious disruption that the construction is likely to bring to Nuortabealli reindeer management is probably insurmountable. (p. 45)

The parliamentary and judicial investigations into the project appeared, for whatever reason, to ignore the detailed evidence and arguments from various sources which Paine summarizes. Both the intrusive project itself, and the apparent official indifference to its effects on reindeer herding, must have been seen by Saami as more than an attack on their economy: it was an assault on their very culture. The area in which they are based in Kautokeino county is quintessentially Saami. Understandably, therefore, the whole episode was symbolically transformed by the Saami into a confrontation between themselves and Norwegians in which the salient issues became those of their ethnic and cultural integrity, and their territorial rights as the aboriginal population of the area. This was not an exaggeration of their plight. If reindeer pastoralism became non-viable and jobs were not available to bolster the household economies of the sedentary population, outmigration — the dissolution of the community — might become the only practicable economic option for the younger generation. Thus, says Paine,

> To inquire about the importance of reindeer pastoralism for Saami culture is like asking about the importance of a right arm to its left — a question one really asks after the left has been amputated.

And, he concludes,

> The population is too small for the culture to survive the amputation . . . The proposed Alta/Kautokeino hydro scheme brings the Saami world in Norway very close indeed to its 'to be or not to be'. The likely consequences are so encompassing. They affect sedentary as well as pastoralist Saami: their ecology, economy, demography and hence their *sense of self as Saami*. (pp. 71, 73, 90)

Quite clearly, then, the Alta project led Saami to a critical confrontation across their ethnic boundary. If they allowed it to be breached this time, it might be breached irreparably. Their ethnicity had earlier been described as 'a spoiled identity' and as a stigma (Eidheim, 1969). They were then portrayed as seeking to mute or wholly conceal their Lappishness when in the presence of non-Lapps. Their attitude seems to have been that of an irredeemably defeated, colonized minority, anachronistic, unsophisticated, and steadily diminishing in number through intermarriage and outmigration. But contemporary reports of their reaction to the Alta plans reveal a dramatic departure from this quiescent posture. Saami pitched a *lavvo* (traditional tent) in front of the Norwegian Parliament in Oslo, from which they conducted a hunger strike. They occupied television studios and forced public discussion of their case. They flaunted their distinctive costume and celebrated their music and language. Thus liberated from stigma, many Norwegians suddenly 'discovered' their Saami antecedents. Protesting Saami tied down half of the nation's police force in the tundra through their campaign of civil disobedience. They burst upon the country's conscience and consciousness. They lost their case in the state courts and legislature, but successfully reconstituted their community and revived its symbolic vitality.

The type of subordination to which the Saami had long been subjected within their 'own' boundaries has been described as one of 'internal colonialism'. More recently such disprivileged and peripheral minorities have been designated 'the fourth world', and strikingly similar strategies of symbolic militancy have been observed among fourth world communities (see, for example, Dyck, 1985). But earlier versions of such symbolic responses were ubiquitous phenomena throughout the colonial 'third world'. One of the most celebrated examples was that of the Melanesian cargo cult. These cults were native movements of protest or incipient rebellion against the colonial power, whose ostensible aims were couched in arcane terms referring to the groups' putative tradition.

'Cargo' was a generic term used to signify extrinsic material and, hence, the intrusive alien power, for the colonial personnel would be supplied by ships from afar carrying all manner of 'cargo': weapons, clothes, months-old copies of the London *Times*, cigarettes, matches and processed foods, and so forth. 'Cargo' symbolized superiority in political, material and military terms. The indigenous population had nothing comparable to pit against such technological sophistication and mighty manufacture. This onslaught of alien values brought tremendous ideological pressure to bear upon the indigenous boundary. Lacking a credible response in comparable terms, one was found from deep within the community's cultural reserves. It, too, had a cargo: not hampers from Fortnum's, but the weight of native doctrine and tradition as embodied symbolically in its religious and ancestral systems. After all the P&O steamers, and ships bearing the white ensign, it was to be the turn of native vessels bearing their cargo: the ancestors. The ancestors' return to the colonized homeland was, in part, a metaphorical state-ment of the eventual triumph of native values over those superimposed upon them, Again, the community would be revivified by the symbolic reassertion of its boundaries against the outside world (see, especially, Worsley, 1967; also Lawrence, 1964; Burridge, 1960).

A comparable, if more pacific reassertion of nativist ideological integrity may be found in the idea of 'négritude', a French African precursor of what was later to sweep the Western world as 'black con-sciousness'. Colonialism brought not only armies and administrators, but also ideas. The language, religion and philosophy of the colonial power displaced or suppressed those of the subject peoples. As we have seen already from the ethnographic material, religious belief does not translate monolithically but, in its vernacular forms, may well become a medium for the expression of nativist ideas. By the same token the literacy of European languages was made into a weapon for the expres-sion of essentially African ideas. The Senegalese poet and president, Leopold Senghor, harnessed the French language to the artistic state-ment of an African consciousness — and thus pioneered the modern 'pirating' of alien art forms, exploiting these imported forms to express 'ardently Africanist' content (Worsley, 1964, p. 119) as a way of bolstering the boundary against its subversion and dissipation by the encroaching culture.

> The African in French Africa, if he was not to evolve into a Frenchman with a black skin, and thereby cut himself off from his own people, had to confront French and European culture much more frontally than those for whom a crude

colour-bar solved the problem. . . This is why négritude developed as a consciously militant creed defining the African much more strongly in French Africa . . . . (Worsley, 1964, p. 119).

Here, then, is a precise illustration of the argument: when the *structural* bases of the boundary are dismantled or become anachronistic – French colonialism lacking the racial segregation of its British counterpart – they are replaced by cultural bases expressed symbolically. If they are not thus replaced, the community disintegrates as a distinctive entity. In the case of négritude, the medium for the symbolic reassertion of the boundary is provided by the very structural form – the French language – whose importation had subverted the old boundary.

An interesting counterpart to the négritude of Francophone Africa was the Africanization of what were imported as European political ideas. One of the most celebrated such cases is the doctrine of 'African socialism' propounded by Julius Nyerere of Tanzania. Nyerere translates the socialization of property into the customary (and, often, apocryphal) corporatism of the tribal and lineage systems, and argues that the modern nation state is merely the old corporate entity writ large. Similarly, he evokes another impressionistic image of traditional tribal society to distinguish the African one-party state from the European dictatorship. Political parties, he argues, are the political expression of antagonistic class interests. But, he claims, African society was traditionally classless and, therefore, competitive political parties are redundant.

This kind of syncretism is a universal feature of culture contact. I have dwelt on it here, not to repeat the obvious observation that it happens but, rather, to suggest one of its implications. It does not just render alien forms into indigenous, and therefore intelligible, idioms. It is not merely an expedient appropriation of the other man's weapons – in the manner of a guerrilla force equipping itself with armour captured from the enemy. Rather, it compensates for any weakening of the boundary which may be caused by structural imports, by bolstering and reinforcing the symbolic statement of the boundary and, therefore, of the terms in which the community can experience a sense of self.

In all these examples we find symbolism reinforcing the cultural boundaries of the community by reconstituting its tradition. In this way communities maintain distinctive meanings for behaviour whose forms they apparently share. Let us underline the argument with two further case studies drawn from very different contexts. They deal with forms of behaviour – Christian burial, and drawing lots – which occur in many different cultural settings and which, therefore, might be assumed to indicate a convergence among them and a weakening or blurring of the boundaries which divide them. However, as we shall see, the conceptual constructions placed upon these forms of behaviour are such as to keep the communities apart as worlds of meaning in the minds of their members.

Case: Burial and exhumation in Potamia

The ritual and symbolism of the ceremonies which attend and follow death have long attracted the attention of anthropologists, not because of any inherently morbid tendencies in the discipline but because the social definition of death casts an instructive light on a society's attitudes to the relationship between the individual and the society as a whole. In some analyses we find the argument that in mortuary rites the symbolic reversal of normal behaviour emphasizes the norm and thus provides a means of stressing continuity. In others, the emphasis is on the metaphorical connections between the life (or death) of an individual and that of society itself. Quite apart from their religious or cosmological significance funerary rites are often an important sociological index of both the deceased and of those by whom they are mourned. The anthropology of death-related practices and beliefs covers a vast and rich literature to which any attempt here at brief summary would be a crude disservice. Our present task is to consider one specific ethnographic case to see what it may tell us of the symbolic construction of the community from which it was drawn.

The religious observance of mortuary rites in rural Greece is conducted within the broad framework of Greek Orthodoxy. However, within this over-arching doctrinal and liturgical form there are substantial variations in practice, and in the meanings imputed to practice. A recently published study looks in detail, textually and photographically, at the celebration of death in Potamia, a village in northern Thessaly. Its six hundred inhabitants are prosperous, if small-scale, farmers. Not unusually, the village has its own well-kept, if very small, graveyard. Also, not unusually for rural Greece, the graves are only temporary resting places for the remains of the dead before they are moved finally to the ossuary. Here,

> Beyond a small floor-space, a ladder led down to a dark, musty-smelling area filled with the bones of many generations of villagers. Near the top of the huge pile the remains of each person were bound up separately in a white cloth. Toward the bottom of the pile the bones — skulls, pelvises, ribs, the long

bones of countless arms and legs — lay in tangled disarray, having lost all trace of belonging to distinct individuals with the disintegration of the cloth wrappings. Stacked in one corner of the building were metal boxes and small suitcases with names, dates, and photographs identifying the people whose bones lay securely within. (Danforth, 1982, pp. 10—11)

Let us examine the transition from interment to exhumation for the symbolic statement of its social significance as a marker of Potamia's sense of collective self.

The duration of this transition is five years, during which mourning obligations and rituals must be observed according to a specified routine. Almost all of these obligations fall on women. Since the ritual despatch of the dead lasts for so long, and any woman may be bound to thus serve parents, spouse, siblings, children, or to assist some other woman, it follows that a substantial proportion of the village's women must be engaged in these duties at any time. Indeed, for a woman in mourning the graveyard becomes an extension of her domestic surroundings. She visits, cleans and tidies the grave daily, a routine which the ethnographer refers to as 'housecleaning' (Danforth, 1982), just as he refers to the grave as a 'home' for the bereaved (p. 15). These visits are made by all the women at the same time of day — shortly after vespers. Their very mourning is itself shared among them, through the serial singing of laments (cf. Du Boulay, 1982). There is a sense in which the five years of interment are a period in which the bereaved woman is withdrawn from the community and normal social intercourse. Many women will leave their houses only to visit the graveyard; should they wish to visit at any other than the usual time, they do so under cover of darkness when literally hidden from the community. They eschew entertainment and socializing, mixing only with close relatives and with the other women mourners (Danforth, 1982, p. 54).

The exhumation, after five years have elapsed, may be regarded as, among other things, a return of both deceased and bereaved to society (p. 60). The customary view, reported by Danforth, is that exhumation is performed so that the deceased might be seen for one last time by their families; so that they 'should not have to bear the weight of the earth . . . for eternity', and so that they might 'see once more the light of the sun' (p. 15). But this folk-religious account is partial and, perhaps, its very literalness hides a cultural metaphor.

Indeed, there are *social* aspects of exhumation. Firstly, the event is inherently social. It is attended by a wide circle of people, spanning the village population. The actual exhumation is carried out by a woman who seems to perform this task frequently, and is closely observed by all in attendance. Secondly, the condition of the remains is interpreted as an indication of the deceased's moral biography. Ideally, body, hair and clothes should be completely decomposed, and the bones should be white. But this moral interpretation rests upon the social knowledge of the deceased and his or her antecedents in the community. Thus, the villagers resolve their puzzlement over the black bones of a young woman, believed to have led a blameless life, by recalling her grandfather who, as a policeman, 'may have testified falsely on occasion or accepted a bribe' (p. 22). Further, the character of the interpretation also appears to reflect the quality of the relationships among those commenting and the deceased's family. For example,

> The relatives and friends of a person whose body did not fully decompose attribute this to natural causes. Those on bad terms with the deceased or his family are eager to lay the blame on any sins he may have committed. (p. 50)

The point is, then, that this ostensibly religious event has a script which is only properly readable by and intelligible to those who share the same idiomatic boundaries — those of the local community itself. It is precisely through their sharing of these idioms that, even in the depths of grief, people become conscious of their co-membership. They contrast their own reading in corporeal decomposition of a person's moral career with the more worldly judgements made in the cities; they contrast their intimate involvement with mortuary rites to the detachment of the professional undertakers and funeral parlours of the sophisticated world beyond their village. The manner in which they dispose of their dead thus speaks to them eloquently of the social context of their lives — their community.

Case: Drawing lots in Cat Harbour

Cat Harbour was an *outport* (village) on the east coast of Newfoundland, the easternmost province of Canada, with a population in 1964 of of 285 (Faris, 1972, p. 41). Like many small Newfoundland settlements the entire community was shortly thereafter relocated to a more populous regional centre. Throughout the community's life Cat Harbour families subsisted on a combination of small-scale agriculture, hunting, fishing, and lumbering. When Faris studied Cat Harbour, the dominant mode of the summer and autumn fishing used the 'trap net', a trap moored in a 'berth' in eight to fifteen fathoms of water (p. 28). The most fruitful berths were generally known in local tradition, and were located by means of the basic triangulation system of 'marks' used throughout northern North Atlantic fishing societies. Even this elementary navigation resonates with community consciousness. Thus, Faris writes,

> a newly-emergent problem in Cat Harbour is the transmission of the precise marks for the many 'spots of ground' to the young. Previously, marks were transmitted orally, and fishermen today are hesitant to write these marks down for fear outsiders will learn them and exploit Cat Harbour waters. (p. 29)

The 'outsider' here does not merely imply competition. Rather, the stranger in Cat Harbour ideology is the personification of much that is fearful and negatively valued. Strangerhood, says Faris, is 'a category edged with suspicion' (p. 135) and is associated with the most unpropitious colour of all, black, which connotes pollution and evil (p. 141). Coming from the world beyond the community's boundaries, the outsider is thus 'hostile' and 'potentially dangerous' (p. 165).

To keep the fishing outsiders at bay, and to avoid any unfair advantage in the allocation of trap berths, the Cat Harbour fishermen had initiated a system of drawing lots for the berths, a device they operated for more than thirty years and which later was incorporated into Federal statutes (p. 47). This kind of balloting is, like Christian burial in the case above, a ubiquitous social form, found in innumerable societies. But clearly its introduction into this vital area of Cat Harbour life did nothing to lessen the distinctive character of the community. Indeed, so heavily did the Cat Harbour fishermen put their idiosyncratic impress upon it that it would be barely recognizable to outsiders. Faris argues that so deeply entrenched is the distrust of authority and leadership that people shy away from any assertive or authoritative action:

> simply making any decisions affecting others is difficult in the traditions of the Cat Harbour moral community. (p. 104)

One might think that in the matter of drawing lots, such decision-making is avoided. But.

> The annual cod-trap berth drawing is a long and agonizing affair, for hours are spent on decisions about just who is to draw for the crew and what berth the person drawing will choose.

So, here we have an ostensibly routine event which has taken place annually for more than thirty years and which, one would therefore suppose, might well be regarded as having so well established a procedure as to be taken for granted. Yet, the near paralysis which it engenders shows that it is not so. The form or structure of the event is irrelevant in itself until rendered into the idiom of the community. It evokes in its participants the fundamental questions of their social identity: 'how do *we* do it? How can we make practical sense of this in Cat Harbour?' Again, the routine event resonates symbolically; the 'technical' act becomes an evocation and statement of community consciousness. Clearly, the imported structure provides a new medium for the recognition and reassertion of the community's boundaries.

This kind of example could be found in profusion within almost any culture. The process which it illustrates is the reconstitution of 'tradition' and the cultural boundary through the use of symbolic devices — specifically by re-rendering structures and forms of behaviour which have originated elsewhere in such a way that they are made congruent with the proclivities of indigenous cognition. Here, then, *structures* transcend the community boundary, but their meanings do not. The boundaries therefore remain intact.

Let us turn now to look at another way in which symbolic behaviour counter-attacks against the threatened subversion by social change of a community's cultural integrity. In this variety, the imported structures are not transformed to anything like the same extent. But their importation is balanced by the modernization of customary symbolic forms to respond to implied change in the community. Often, these updated forms come to have characters which differ in meaning and importance from their appearance.

APPEARANCES ARE DECEPTIVE

We have been discussing the differences between 'structure' and 'meaning' — a distinction which we have also expressed as between form and substance. In the preceding section, we saw that the latter category can be independent of the former: that substance is *not* determined by form, and that therefore the kind of social change which brings new forms or structures into a community does not necessarily alter it in any substantial way. But, moreover, there are circumstances in which the *form* of behaviour is used to conceal its substance. Typically, these may occur where a community has adopted much of the structural *appearance* of other communities but nevertheless contrives to preserve a strong sense of distinctive self.

Case: Kizb

One of the more exotic ways in which this is done is through deception or lying, a behavioural strategy which has been well documented by students of Mediterranean societies. For example, the multi-faceted Arabic concept of deception, *kizb,* apparently has the effect of bolstering (rather than subverting) social relations in a north Lebanese village. According to its ethnographer, the masking of reality and its short-term or superficial distractions, contributes to the maintenance of social relations in their customary form over the longer term. It reconciles ethos (that which people believe *ought* to be) with actuality (that which *is*). Moreover, it is widely accepted within the village as a proper mode of behaviour and discourse (see Gilsenan, 1976, pp. 191–219). This argument recalls earlier anthropological theories of myth in which myth is displayed as resolving the tensions which ensue from the apparent contradictions between belief and practice (e.g. Lévi-Strauss, 1963; Leach, 1968).

Were we to apply this view of lying to our argument, we could formulate some such hypothesis as: the lie maintains customary meaning by keeping at bay the change implied in new forms of behaviour. But, of course, the 'lie' (*kizb*) is itself precisely a manifestation of indigenous belief battling against the new and unfamiliar; and it is expressly seen as such:

> it is only in fact by *kizb* that social life can go on at all and the group's fragile corporateness be preserved ... *Kizb* bridges the gap between form and substance, ethos and the actualities of the political economy, but at the same time men directly experience and *know* that it is a false 'solution' to the problem. (Gilzeman, 1976, pp. 211–13)

Case: The Alcalá lie

Kizb thus symbolizes the boundary. In a celebrated anthropological study lying is presented as an expression of people's sensitivity to their community and its boundaries. In *The people of the Sierra,* Pitt-Rivers (1971) describes the villagers of 'Alcalá', and of the other communities in the Andalusian sierra, as intensely committed partisans of their own localities, a commitment which also implies antagonism to neighbouring localities: the very sentiment of boundary-consciousness which we have discussed above. This partisanship and its corresponding rivalries are expressed in nicknaming, in patronal cults, in folklore and popular histories, in occasional violence, in variations in material culture (Pitt-Rivers, 1971, pp. 8–13). In such a highly-charged milieu, the capacity to lie — or, at least, to disguise and keep secret the truth from prying eyes — is an essential social and communal weapon:

> the Andalusians are the most accomplished liars I have ever
> encountered. . . . it requires training and intelligence to distin-
> guish rapidly when the truth is owed and when it is to be
> concealed . . . we are all fumblers by Andalusian standards . . .
> (pp. xvi–xvii)

But this practised deceit is not motivated by contempt for the truth:
precisely the contrary:

> it is logical rather than paradoxical that the Andalusians
> should be people profoundly concerned with the truth and
> with the true state of the heart. . . . when knowledge is some-
> thing to give or to deny you become concerned with its exact
> worth . . . . (p. xvii)

For the Alcalareños, just as for the members of the neighbouring villages,
the 'truth' is in their sense of the qualities which distinguish their village
from the others and which give the lie to their apparent similarity. It
is this sense above all other factors which keeps them apart. As we
noted earlier, the need to emphasize cultural and ideological difference
varies inversely with differences of scale and structure. The communal
sense of distinctiveness and commitment to the village is underpinned
by the tradition of plebian solidarity in the Andalusian *pueblo* (p. 18),
and by a sharp sensitivity to public opinion engendered within the
pueblo. It is,

> a unity derived from physical and moral proximity, common
> knowledge and the acceptance of common values. (p. 31)

The sense of community in Alcalá is built upon the dialectical
interplay of internal and external pressures which has fascinated anthropologists and sociologists for so long. The members of a community
recognize their common interests and values *vis-à-vis* those of other
communities. But, at the same time, they cherish their differences from
each other for, to a substantial extent, these provide the very stuff of
everyday social life within the community. But the two are clearly
linked. I have argued above that people's perception of their community *as a whole* is mediated by the particularities of their membership of it. For example,

Pitt-Rivers argues that the tensions which inhere potentially in *intra*-community differentiation become externalized and thereby reinforce the solidarity of the group as a whole. The lie is one of the devices used to conceal from the outsider the reality of dissensus within a community. But the common ability of insiders to 'read' a lie nudges them into consciousness of their co-membership and, by implication, of the outsider's exclusion. Moreover, the lie, quite apart from being honorific if well-perpetrated, may effectively mask the degree of internal conflict and thereby help to preserve the sense of commonality. Lying is, *par excellence,* an example of behaviour which has both pragmatic or instrumental *and* symbolic efficacy. We will return to Alcalá later.

The kind of deceit involved in *kizb* and in the Alcalá lie are extreme and explicit forms of behaviour which preserve a certain cultural order through deliberate distortion. But symbolic life is replete with behaviour which similarly expresses social values whilst masquerading as a means to some much more specific end.

Case: Thuic
The Dinka are a pastoral people who live around the swamps of the central Nile basin in the southern Sudan. The richness of their ritual life is matched by the complexity of their pantheon, and both complement their intricate tribal organization. Their quintessential symbolic act, built upon the whole symbolic edifice, is animal sacrifice. But one of the most intriguing, if minor, elements of this edifice is *thuic*:

> The practice called *thuic* involves knotting a tuft of grass to indicate that the one who makes the knot hopes and intends to contrive some kind of constriction or delay. (Lienhardt, 1961, p. 282)

For example, to knot an enemy in grass would be to express the wish that his freedom of action might be restricted in some way. Or,

> When Dinka are making a journey, they often tie knots in the grass growing beside the path with the intention that the preparation of food at the end of the journey may be delayed until their arrival. (*ibid.*)

But it would be quite wrong to infer that Dinka believed in the efficacy of a mystical connection between the performance of this act and the desired result, the kind of connection which we are invited to impute to the magician's spell and his trick. Indeed, says Lienhardt,

> No Dinka thinks that by performing such an action he has actually assured the result he hopes for.

It is not so unambiguously a technical or instrumental action. Rather, *thuic* — the symbolic act — is 'a complement to . . . and preparation for' instrumental action:

> The man who ties such a knot has made an external, physical representation of a well-formed mental intention. He has produced a model of his desires and hopes, upon which to base renewed practical endeavour. (p. 283)

The purpose of the symbolic act is thus not to induce magically a reaction in someone else, but to induce or sustain a state of mind in its perpetrator. Thus, when bedouin sacrifice an animal to mark the healing of some social breach, it is not to assist mystically in repairing the rupture. Rather, it consecrates the reconciliation in the minds of its participants: it marks the transformation of social relations as being significant (Peters, 1984). When Englishmen shake hands on first meeting, their bodily contact does not indicate any special intimacy, allegiance or commitment. It simply marks the occasion as one of the initial meeting between them. It has no more significance than that. But when friends who have quarrelled with each other shake hands after resolving their dispute, the joining of their hands clearly does symbolize a re-making of the bond between them. The symbolic act is not merely for public consumption; the public may not even be involved. It is, rather, 'to control . . . a set of mental and moral dispositions' and, as evidence for this contention, Lienhardt adds that, in taking such action, 'there is no purely technical alternative . . .' (p. 283).

Now, I should not wish to claim that the Dinka practice of *thuic* has any cultural self-consciousness about it; it is certainly not in this sense that Lienhardt presents it to us. But it is reasonable to suppose that in circumstances of culture contact (with neighbouring tribesmen, such as Nuer and Azande, and with the British colonial administration) such apparently routine symbolic acts do serve as a cultural mnemonic, a sense of cultural identity being among the 'mental dispositions' which they induce. For example, Lienhardt tells us that,

> a Dinka who could send a message by the driver of some car going on ahead of him would not find it necessary to knot grass when hoping that supper might be kept for him.

Dinka do not see the motorized message and *thuic* as mere instrumental alternatives. Lienhardt says each course of action has a different competence. But each must also be seen as pertaining to different cultural modes of action: if the tribesman stops the car, it is as if he says to himself, 'I will use *their* device'; if he knots grass, 'I will use ours.' Indeed, the burden of Lienhardt's seminal discussion of Dinka ritual life is precisely that ritual transforms experience. Discussing *thuic*, Douglas argues that ritual 'frames' action in such a way as to enable us to experience what might otherwise not be disclosed to us. Ritual, she says, '. . . can permit knowledge of what would otherwise not be known at all' (Douglas, 1966, p. 64).

And what might 'otherwise not be known' or experienced is awareness of the boundary and consciousness of the community. Here, then, the ritual responds to changed circumstances and has a vital competence different from and incidental to its ostensible purpose.

Through these cases we have seen another answer to our question of why symbolism is so prominent a medium for the assertion of community boundaries. The very versatility of symbolic form and its capacity to obscure indigenous realities from those on 'the other side' of the boundary protects those realities from subversion by change and intrusion.

APPEARANCE AND TRANSFORMATION

To conclude this chapter, let us look at one further characteristic of symbolism which provides yet another clue to its ubiquitous use in the defence of boundaries, particularly in circumstances of substantial change. Symbolism owes its versatility to the fact that it does not carry meaning inherently. A corollary of this is that it can be highly responsive to change. As we have seen, symbolic form has only a loose relation to its content. Therefore, the form can persist while the content undergoes significant transformation. Frequently, the *appearance* of continuity is so compelling that it obscures people's recognition that the form itself has changed. The great rituals of the non-industrialized world do not have the stultified and arcane character of grand ceremonial in Britain. Much of our state ceremonial has been frozen in obscure historical form so that we require specialist commentators to interpret it for us. The very choreography of the ceremonial, and its subjection to the discipline of the television camera, have the consequence that we view the event for its aesthetic values rather than for its meaning. This kind of ceremonial performance has become an artificial and unconvincing symbolic form. But this is not true of all of our ritual, nor of ritual and symbolic processes elsewhere.

We saw in the previous chapter that the fantasy which characterizes some rituals may be regarded as a harmless speculation about alterations to the social structure. To this we may now add a further competence of fantasy: that it permits deeply entrenched customary symbolic forms to be used in radically changed circumstances. It thereby *manages* change so that it limits the disruption of people's orientations to their community, and enables them to make sense of novel circumstances through the use of familiar idioms.

I remarked above that students of social behaviour have long recognized people's need to resolve the contradictions between their beliefs and actuality, and that much of the work which anthropologists of various theoretical persuasions have done on myth has focused on precisely this issue. It has been argued that this kind of reconciliation also lies at the heart of religious and ideological belief systems. In all these forms symbolism − and, especially, ritual − is the mechanism which bridges the gap. The disruption caused by social change might be seen as a particular instance of the disjunction between the ideal and the actual: one in which the ideal takes the guise of the 'familiar', and actuality appears as the unfamiliar and, therefore, the feared and/or resented. Here, too, symbolic forms can massage away the tension.

Case: The Buryat Mongols and their Soviet commissars

The Buryat Mongols, studied by Caroline Humphrey (1983), are citizens of the Soviet Union who live in the south-east of Siberia, close to the northern border of Mongolia. They are constituted by a complex mixture of different ethnic, linguistic and religious groups. Nevertheless, they now have in common a view of themselves in relation to the wider society, based upon,

> their sense of a common historical fate, their oral traditions of myth and legend, their genealogical conception of society, their deep concern for kinship relations, their ideas about time and the seasons, their concepts of right and proper behaviour, their respect for animals and often tender care for them, and their love of nature − even that seemingly barren landscape of dry, grey steppes, marshes rimmed with salt, and dank, decaying, mosquito-ridden forest which surround them. (Humphrey, 1983, p. 25)

Their ritual calendar was customarily fundamental to their economic life, a relationship now undermined by the state's 'commandeering' of production, marked by the superimposition of its own ritual calendar. Clearly, the Soviet influence on Buryat ritual behaviour is but one indication of the fundamental transformations which ensued from the incorporation of the Buryats into the Soviet state. Not the least of these has been their transition from nomadic pastoralism to a sedentary life on the huge collective farms.

However, the extent to which Soviet ritual has actually replaced the pre-existing Buryat shamanistic rituals is open to question. Humphrey argues that by an unwitting irony the intrusion of the State might have revived traditional forms, since it displaced not 'Buryat ritual' but, rather, the Buddhist and Orthodox forms imposed upon it. As a consequence and notwithstanding its syncretic integration with Soviet forms, 'Unacknowledged, and often opposed, by the Soviet authorities, the ritual of Buryat folk culture has continued everywhere' (pp. 373–4). The rituals may have become secularized and, in other ways, admitted the influence of Soviet protocols. Yet, the practitioners of ritual,

> attempt to make sense of the disjunction between local or personal problems and a social system which claims to be able to solve them, but which itself . . . presents people regularly with the dilemma of having to act 'in the interests of society' when their own concerns are frequently quite different. (p. 375)

Some rituals, like the *Tsagaalgan* celebration of purity, spring, the renewal of dairy stock, and kinship, are not recognized at all by the Soviet authorities (p. 378). This ritual, as an occasion for the explicit acknowledgement of one's kin, and of the cardinal features of traditional Buryat economic and subsistence life, might also be regarded as an expression of the primacy of people's attachment to their Buryat identity. Such expression might also be found in their other characteristic ritual forms as well, such as weddings. Here the state has made a deliberate attempt to intervene, proposing an official 'komsomol' alternative to the customary form. Yet, Humphrey reports that of approximately forty-five weddings on the Karl Marx Kolkhoz between 1964 and 1967, only two had been of the komsomol type (p. 391). Of course, the traditional ritual form undergoes marked change, reflecting both altered circumstances and the ideological influence of the state. But, nevertheless, there remains a manifest consciousness that the form being observed *is* traditional. It therefore provides a powerful means of reiterating the local and ethnic boundary. Thus, although the old conventions of brideprice may have given way, and the former obeisance to senior males been discontinued; and even though kolkhoz officials may have replaced kin elders as honorific actors in ritual drama (p. 399), there remains a strong awareness that, at least part of what is celebrated is 'Buryat-ness'. This sense of collective self may have been transformed to render intelligible the enormous changes which have overtaken Buryat society (p. 438). Yet, its efficacy in this regard has brought about its regeneration (p. 442).

The similar use of ostensibly customary symbolic forms to manage the disruptive consequences of social change have been widely observed also in studies of British rural communities. In these, as in the examples cited above, the symbolic expression of community is called for by the blurring or weakening of the community's structural boundaries. Hence, the correlation between social change and the incidence of symbolic performance. The nature of these symbolic expressions varies considerably. In the case of Elmdon, referred to earlier, it takes the form of an idiom, phrased in terms of kinship, to invert what are perceived as mainstream British values and thereby expresses the distinctiveness of the indigenous population against the newcomers (Strathern, 1981; 1982a and b). The symbolic demarcation of 'local' and 'incomer' or 'offcomer' appears to be prominent also in inland areas of northern England (see, for example, Rapport, 1983; Phillips, 1984) and much further north in the British Isles (e.g. Forsythe, 1984; McFarlane, 1981; Cohen, 1982a). Elsewhere language differences may crystallize sentiments of class and close social association, as well as those of national and cultural integrity (e.g. Emmett, 1964, 1982; Mewett, 1982). Even the fraught religious sectarianism of Northern Ireland expresses much more complex sensibilities and attachments than those of religious persuasion (Leyton, 1974; Larsen, 1982a and b). It is pertinent to repeat an earlier observation: it is the very versatility and malleability of symbolism which makes it so effective and ubiquitous a means of expressing the distinctiveness – the boundedness – of community. Thus, we find gender divisions in Devon farming families encapsulating not only the organization of domestic labour, but also the idealized image of indigenous farming culture as opposed to that of metropolitan Britain (Bouquet, 1981). Similarly, the resonances of crofting maintain a sharp sense of cultural continuity among the Whalsay Islanders of Shetland, in spite of the massive changes which have transformed island life – *including* crofting – since the Second World War (Cohen, 1979).

Case: The Whalsay spree: continuity of form – transformation of meaning
We conclude this chapter on a celebratory note, looking at the Whalsay spree as a symbolic form whose content has been transformed but whose continuity masks or limits the trauma of change (see Cohen, 1985).

The spree is, essentially, a peripatetic party which moves from house to house, collecting the occupants of one to proceed to the next. They are held on several fixed festive occasions such as Christmas,

New Year and the summer Regatta, after weddings, on the *settling* (accounting) days of the fishing crews, and following other major social events in the community. The spree is traditional in form. It provides an occasion to reunite the community by cutting across the boundaries and divisions which inform everyday social life and by re-stating the principle of access to all local households. Much of the yarning about 'the aald days' recalls notable sprees of the past in which peculiarly parochial values are celebrated: the characteristic brand of Whalsay humour, centering on the shared knowledge of personalities, lore and the locality. The spree always has a household as its venue. In the past, when Whalsay families wrested their livelihood from a variety of subsistence activities — fishing, crofting, peat-cutting, knitting — a livelihood limited by their own resourcefulness, the household was an economic unit in itself, but was also an integral element in a wider collaborative group based upon kinship and neighbourhood. This nexus formed the basic element of a social organization and commitment (see Cohen, 1982b); it still retains its affective primacy, but its salience as a basis for social action has been diminished by the transition to occupational specialization based upon capital-intensive fishing, and by the demise of crofting as an important element of the domestic economy.

For men, day-to-day life is now lived more among one's crew-mates than among one's close kin. The proliferation of crews and the scarcity of capital have considerably diminished the old pattern of kin-based crews. For women, life is far more mobile than was previously the case, since the motor car, the fish factory and the centralization of shopping have broken the woman's seasonal confinement to the crofting township, the peat hill, and the herring station. The proliferation of spheres of social life, and the displacement of kinsfolk and neighbours by 'friends' and work-mates has broken the old structural foundations of the kin-neighbourhood grouping.

Yet, its symbolic potency and its status of primacy in social cognition, is now expressed in the spree. Previously, the kin-neighbourhood group was secure in its geographical and genealogical definitions and its economic function. The spree therefore asserted the value of the wider community through its internal segments. Nowadays, the reverse is true: the community itself is the socioeconomic niche, and the spree expresses the ideological primacy of its segments. There is no contradiction between the idea of community-as-a-whole, and of loyalty to its parts, since people quite clearly understand and perceive the community through the mediation of its parts: they belong to Whalsay *through* their close kin and neighbours, despite the decreased economic saliency of these mediating elements.

As in the past, the spree takes people beyond the social confines of their day-to-day lives, although these confines have clearly changed. Today, the spree takes them *back* to their kinship-neighbourhood group of origin. A spreer's journey may begin anywhere, though the point of origin is often habitual rather than random. His destination at midnight will be a house he customarily frequents at this time on a spree night. The company gathered there, without explicit invitation, invariably represents important reference points on the map of the hosts' close social relationships: it is composed of close kin, neighbours in the past or the present, perhaps close associates of their deceased parents, and so forth. When this climatic phase of the spree is over, the hardy spreer will often walk back to his natal household some miles distant, or to a house with which he was closely associated in childhood or youth (see Cohen, 1982b). Kinship and descent in Whalsay are bilateral and cognatic, with no general bias to either parental side. On marriage, the obligation to balance both sides of one's consanguineal kinship have added to them similar obligations to one's affines. This balance is tested by the need for at least one of the spouses to leave their natal household. The spree provides an occasion to reassert one's primordial loyalties under the licence of the exceptional event. It is a suspension of normal convention and, as such, is often marked by tolerance of drunkenness and a relaxation of the normal discipline of constrained and inhibited behaviour.

Perhaps, like some of those other ritual occasions discussed earlier which suspend normality, the spree is a kind of fantasy in which participants harmlessly speculate on what life would be like if it was other than it is! But leaving aside the niceties of this kind of analysis, it provides us with a precise example of symbolic behaviour which exhibits continuity of form and substantial change of content refracting changed circumstances. Whalsay people conceptualize the community differently now, although they still assert its distinctiveness and, therefore, the reality of its cultural boundary; and they still commit themselves to it. The spree is a symbolic expression of both change and commitment.

4

The Symbolic Construction
of Community

COMMUNITY AS A MENTAL CONSTRUCT

In the Ituri rain forest of Zaire, there lived the Mbuti pygmies, a people marvellously adapted spiritually and organizationally to the nomadic hunting and gathering existence appropriate to the tropical forest. The Mbuti, we are told, had a highly refined idea of peace, *ekimi,* which incorporated the notions of oneness with nature, of social harmony, of egalitarianism, of what might be regarded as a Platonic sense of place and duty. Around them lived Bira villagers: sedentary cultivators, hierarchical, superstitious, fearful of the gods and of the malign forest, argumentative, dependent, credulous — repositories of disharmony, of noise and crisis, *akami.* The Mbuti and the Bira farmers are thus presented as opposite in almost every respect. The Mbuti seek the perfect equilibrium of life at the idealized centre of their sphere; the villagers, by contrast, have no such sense of perfection. Their sphere is biased, wobbling out of control, *waziwazi.* (See Turnbull, 1961, 1983.)

Yet in spite of their contrary characters the Mbuti and Bira are co-participants in a great initiation ritual, *nkumbi,* which federates all the inhabitants of the Ituri. Nkumbi was held every three years. Its ostensible ritual purpose was the circumcision of male initiates, but not the least of its accomplishments was its aggregation of these two strongly contrasting cultures into a collaborative relationship. One interpretation of this ritual might be to regard it as a culturally neutral event, into which both Mbuti and the Bira villagers can move without compromising their respective communities. However, this would be to suppose that the ritual and its symbolism contain inherent meaning: that it constitutes a community in itself. Such an interpretation is implausible. People cannot strip themselves of their cultural equipment to step socially naked into neutral space. Rather, they view it, interpret it, from their own cultural perspectives. The process is similar to the ways in which, we have argued, people interpret symbols: they impute meaning to them in the light of their own experience and purposes. So it is also in *nkumbi*. Whilst Mbuti and the Bira villagers 'share' the ritual form, they do not share its meanings:

> the Nkumbi illustrates . . . the complete opposition of the forest to the village. The pygmies consciously and energetically reject all village values in the forest. . . . there is an unalterable gulf between the two worlds of the two people. (Turnbull, 1961, p. 204).

Like the ethnographies in the preceding chapters, *nkumbi* shows us that culture — the community as experienced by its members — does not consist in social structure or in 'the doing' of social behaviour. It inheres, rather, in 'the thinking' about it. It is in this sense that we can speak of the community as a symbolic, rather than a structural, construct. In seeking to understand the phenomenon of community we have to regard its constituent social relations as repositories of meaning for its members, not as a set of mechanical linkages. Meaning, of course, is ethnographically problematic. It is not susceptible to objective description, but only to interpretation. In this matter we can only aspire to informed speculation. Community exists in the minds of its members, and should not be confused with geographic or sociographic assertions of 'fact'. By extension, the distinctiveness of communities and, thus, the reality of their boundaries, similarly lies in the mind, in the meanings which people attach to them, not in their structural forms. As we have seen, this reality of community is expressed and embellished symbolically.

SYMBOLIZING THE PAST

Much of the ethnography we have reviewed — for example, the Huichol peyote hunt, the Naskapi *mokoshan,* the Whalsay spree, the Buryat wedding, the Melanesian cargo cults — shows that this symbolic expression of community refers to a putative past or tradition. We thus encounter the paradox that, although the re-assertion of community is made necessary by contemporary circumstances, it is often accomplished through precisely those idioms which these circumstances threaten with redundancy.

It would be a mistake, though, to characterize such responses as merely 'traditionalistic', implying that the community in question is mired in its own past and is unable to face up to present imperatives. Rather, the past is being used here as a resource, in a number of ways. The manner in which the past is invoked is strongly indicative of the kinds of circumstance which makes such a 'past-reference' salient. It is a selective construction of the past which resonates with contemporary influences. Sometimes this kind of folk history resembles myth, or meta-history, in the sense which Malinowski gave to the word: a 'charter' for contemporary action whose legitimacy derives from its very association with the cultural past. Myth confers 'rightness' on a course of action by extending to it the sanctity which enshrouds tradition and lore. Mythological distance lends enchantment to an otherwise murky contemporary view. One reason which accounts for the particular efficacy of myth in this regard is its a-historical character. As one writer has put it, myth is 'beyond time'. It 'blocks off' the past, making it impervious to the rationalistic scrutiny of historians, lawyers and others who may dispute precedent and historiographical validity (P. S. Cohen, 1969).

Historians have recently described this process as the 'invention of tradition'. Anthropologists tend not to impute such a contrived character to it. They would be more inclined to treat myth as an expression of the way in which people cognitively map past, present and future. In the struggle to interpret, we use our past experience to render stimuli into a form sufficiently familiar that we can attach some sense to them. Our experience functions as, what Geertz called (1966), a 'model of' reality. Without such models, we should have no basis from which to orient ourselves to the phenomenon requiring interpretation. When we find ourselves unable to thus render the unknown into some familiar form, we tend to become frightened. Societies experience similar collective responses: the collective heart begins to thump and, if the flow of adrenalin in not curtailed, crisis and disruption may well ensue. But, of course, everyday life is full of potential crises: decisions to be made, arguments averted, social interaction successfully negotiated. Usually we are able to defuse, or neutralize, the crisis by deploying our models of reality — 'common sense' models which we use, as Geertz observes (1983, p. 79), like the Azande 'second spear' of witchcraft: to explain what would otherwise be inexplicable. That these crises only seldom materialize is testimony to the deftness of the models. As Geertz's prosaic metaphor puts it, 'Men plug the dikes of their most needed beliefs with whatever mud they can find' (Geertz, 1983, p. 80). When such *bricolage* fails we are in trouble. The boy's invitation to a girl to dance will be met, he supposes, by polite acceptance or refusal. Indeed, his invitation is based upon this assumption. But if she replies instead with a kick on the shin, he is likely to be somewhat disconcerted. He must then do what we do not normally need to do: *consider* his response, because his common sense models do not extend to this contingency. A similar, if less traumatic confusion may result when an enquiry about directions made to someone in the street elicits a verbal stream of consciousness in a foreign language. We stumble and bumble and eventually move away, probably with a slightly less than civil demeanour.

Usually we try to pour oil on the troubled waters of social interaction-gone-awry. Goffman, in *Interaction Ritual* (1967), gives the example of two pedestrians approaching from opposite directions, attempting to avoid each other, but colliding as if magnetically attracted. Yet, instead of giving free rein to their understandable anger, people involved in such incidents often apologize to each other, regardless of their conviction that the fault really lay with the other person. The alternative could be a fundamental breakdown of the orderliness which underpins normal social interaction.

The familiar, orderliness, is invoked to inject sense into the unfamiliar. Often, also, the invocation of the familiar is so intuitive, so unguarded a reaction, that it can get in the way of understanding. Chapman reports his difficulty, as an Englishman, in mastering the conventions of handshaking in Brittany. Recalling his consternation at the frequency of handshaking and the ubiquity of kissing, he also divulges the confusion he must have sown by his failure to remember those with whom he had already shaken hands on any given day, having, therefore, to resort to shaking hands repeatedly with the same people and, thereby, appearing 'oddly tempered'. He reveals further difficulties. If a fisherman was unable to proffer a hand because it was too dirty, he would, 'offer what can only be described as his shoulder', since a left hand, even if clean and pristine, is not acceptable as a substitute for the right. But, having injured his own right hand,

> I was anxious to avoid anybody's gripping me by the right
> hand, and so tended to hold it back. What I *should* have done
> was offer my right forearm. Because, however, I come from a
> culture where handshaking is not particularly important, and

certainly not important enough to drive the classificatory hand right up to the shoulder in circumstances where the 'hand' itself was injured or otherwise unavailable, I shook hands far less than I should have. The Englishman was 'reserved'. Once or twice, purely on impulse, when I was faced with an unavoidable handshake, I offered a curiously twisted left hand; this was, to judge from the expression that clouded the face of the recipient, a very strange thing to do. Not only 'reserved', then, but rather odd with it. (Chapman, 1982, p. 136).

With their proffered hands, each party also extends its own customary idioms or models to render the scenario familiar in order that each can act upon it. That their models are dissonant may be immaterial to them. But it is instructive for us since it underlines the ubiquity of the process.

So if the individuals refer to their cognitive maps to orient themselves in interaction, the same is true also of collectivities. The maps are part of their cultural store, accumulated over generations and, thus, heavily scented by the past.

For most people, at most moments of history, the past is inchoate, transmitted only selectively according to contemporary purposes, and recalled selectively without historiographical rigour. It inheres in such undiscriminating categories as 'the old days', 'when I was young', 'in our ancestors' time'. History is wonderfully malleable, whether in the hands of academic historians or of laymen. Even without the intention to distort, its recollection always rests upon interpretive reconstructions. Collingwood's Weberian injunction to historians to get 'inside' historical events by replicating the mentality of those who populated them can only result, at best, in the exercise of informed imagination. But folk uses of history rarely require even this attempt to distance oneself from the present. Quite the reverse, they more often conflate past and present. Even those folk histories which take an apparently precise form, such as genealogies, are continually revised in such a way as to bend to present needs (see, for example, Fox, 1982; Cohen and Comaroff, 1976; Fortes 1970). In our everyday discourse, the past, itself symbolic, is recalled to us symbolically. Simple 'historical' labels are made to describe complex and often ideological messages. We are most used to this in political rhetoric. For example, Menachem Begin, sometime prime minister of Israel, effectively deployed the tenuous historical figments of Judaea and Samaria to articulate and legitimate the expansionist territorial ambitions of Israel in the 1970s (see, for example, Oz, 1983). Margaret Thatcher used the simplistic artifice of

Islam

'Victorian values' to lend credence and ethical validity to economic monetarism. The Ayatollah Khomeini, President Zia and Colonel Qadafi have all, in their various ways, invoked a supposedly traditional Islam to justify their extremist modern nationalisms. But in this, as in most matters, the politicians only write large the strategic behaviour of ordinary people in less elevated social positions. When parents berate their children for insolence and, by contrast, recall their own respectful behaviour to *their* parents, they are doing a Thatcher. When people quarrel over possession, invoking precedents of previous occupancy, they do a Begin. In these cases, they go beyond the presentation of precise comparison between past and present. There is more being conveyed and recollected than a child's demeanour to his father. Rather, the recollection is of a way of life, of complex characters, of a large fabric of values and attitudes. The emblematic use of Queen Victoria, of divine promises and injunctions, and of the Fifth Commandment, all précis much more complicated stories and messages into a mnemonic or shorthand form.

Such mnemonics which trigger an emotional response or attitude are termed by Turner, following Freud and Sapir, as 'condensation symbols'. Through their use, 'Norms and values, on the one hand, become saturated with emotion, while the gross and basic emotions become ennobled through contact with social values' (Turner, 1967, p. 30). Symbols of the 'past', mythically infused with timelessness, have precisely this competence, and attain particular effectiveness during periods of intensive social change when communities have to drop their heaviest cultural anchors in order to resist the currents of transformation. An illustration may be found once more from the Shetland island community of Whalsay.

As remarked earlier, Whalsay's social and economic life changed substantially during the 1960s and 1970s, with very large investments being made in capital-intensive fishing technology, with a consequent specialization of labour and diminution of the earlier plural sources of income and subsistence. Yet, crofting clearly remained salient and highly valued, although the financial returns it offered to even the most assiduous part-time crofter were, at best, marginal. To most Whalsay fishermen, the croft represented costs in labour and cash that could hardly be justified in economic terms. To add to this apparent anomaly, the only type of crofting agriculture which is at all practicable in these circumstances is that of sheep husbandry — a mode in which, at the time, few Whalsay crofters were skilled. Nevertheless, there remained a continuous demand for crofts and great interest in people's crofting performance (see Cohen, 1979).

of farming

The apparent paradox may be resolved by seeing crofting and its associated activities as being more then merely economic, as having in addition a powerful symbolic dimension which 'condenses' a sense of the valued past and the continuity of tradition even in the much-changed present. For example, there has been a remarkable stability in the domiciliary locations of Whalsay families over more than three hundred years, and this has been further underpinned by legislative reforms in crofting tenure. The croft, then, is not just an arena of labour, but is also family territory with long historical associations. As such it is a fundamental referent of identity (Cohen, 1979, p. 259). With such a compelling basis in social and physical space, it becomes plausible to see the croft as a symbolic resource through which, during a period of intensive change, social identity can be stabilized. Crofting,

> is a way both of masking the cultural distance which has been travelled, and of reinforcing commitment to the ideals of the community. (Cohen, 1979, p. 263).

Moreover,

> it is an activity whose past is still available, both physically and through lore. Croft boundaries have remained fairly stable over the years and old boundary divisions, such as turf walls, are still to be seen. The *crubs* (circular stone enclosures within which seedling plants were grown) of traditional cultivation are still dotted all over the island, though few are still in use. There still remain old croft houses, many now considerably enlarged and renovated. Parts of crofts are still known by their associations of generations ago — 'Annie's toon', 'Eppie's Yard', 'the whaley midden dyke'. Thus, the 'cultural map' of the crofting community has not changed, as houses, crofts, parts of crofts, rocks, dykes, hills, inlets, holms and skerries are still designated by names whose origins lie far back in the mists of time. There is, thereby, a tangible sense that the same paths have been trodden, the same ditches cleared, the same boundaries maintained for generations past . . . The croft is the repository of that valued tradition in which resides the idea of community. (*ibid.*, p. 263). *archetype*

So, it is the very imprecision of these references to the past — timelessness masquerading as history — which makes them so apt a device for symbolism and, in particular, for expressing symbolically the continuity of past and present, and for re-asserting the cultural integrity of the community in the face of its apparent subversion by the forces of change.

RESPONDING TO THE PRESENT: ETHNICITY AND LOCALITY

However, it is obviously the case that not all communities are so resilient, and not all make such a determined and vibrant response to change. Many become deserted, culturally and/or demographically (see, for example, Brody, 1973], or are wholly transformed, losing their sense of themselves or suffering its debasement through the fetishization of its material objects (see, Helias, 1979; also, Smith, 1981, pp. 156ff). The question therefore arises: what produces such vehemence and assertiveness? The answer can only be given in general terms, with no suggestion that similar circumstances will invariably evoke a similar response in different communities. The answer has not often been attempted in respect of local communities. The most instructive available precedents relate to the political assertion of culture difference — a phenomenon generally described through the somewhat abused label of 'ethnicity' (see Paine, 1977, 1985).

The inclination of an 'ethnic' group to assert its cultural integrity is clearly stimulated by more than just a well-developed collective self-consciousness. Many of the examples we have encountered above show that it follows from more than mere contrast with other groups. Often, it seems to follow from a sense of disadvantage, or subordination — but then many disadvantaged and subordinated groups go under. Anthony Smith suggests that the revival of ethnicity in Europe re-activated an earlier ethnic consciousness dating back over two or more centuries (1981, pp. 20ff). Interesting though this observation may be, it does not explain why the 'revival' occurred as and when it did. Part of the answer may lie in the suggestion that Paine makes with regard to the Kautokeino Saami, when he writes of them reaching their 'to be or not to be' (*Supra*, p. 79). The implication is that when groups feel they have nothing more to lose than their sense of self, then they cast caution to the winds and confront the dominant nationalisms and statisms. But there must be more to it than this for, whilst ethnic activism may be fashionable, it is nevertheless more of a thorn in the flesh, than a stake through the heart of the great polities. Indeed, one of the most authoritative, if controversial writers on the subject is inclined to dismiss the widespread assertiveness of the 1960s and 1970s as merely 'an ethnic binge':

> The very word 'ethnicity' was coined during that period. It became fashionable to discover, cultivate and cuddle 'ethnic identities' and 'roots' . . . All of a sudden, social scientists began to proclaim that the melting pot had failed and had been a sham to start with, that ethnic identities were precious,

that assimilationism was a sinister policy of 'ethnocide', and that the state should give full recognition to ethnic and racial sentiments and should base its policies of resource distribution on criteria of race and ethnicity. (van den Berghe, 1981, p. 4)

Whilst he stresses the sociobiological basis of the 'ethny' in endogamy and extended kinship, van den Berghe also sees ethnicity as a strategy, based upn choice and informed by a calculus of advantage (1981, pp. 254ff). But he turns the problem of ethnicity on its head by making ethnic primacy the norm, and assimilation the aberration which therefore requires analysis. For example, 'ethnicity is more primordial than classs. Blood runs thicker than money' (1981, p. 243). In this regard it is the very 'irrationality' of ethnicity which makes its sentiments so powerful and so readily aroused:

Appeals to ethnic sentiments need no justification other than common 'blood'. They are couched in terms of 'our people' versus 'them'. (*ibid.*)

and are most easily mobilized if 'them' can be depicted as posing a threat to 'us'.

The persuasiveness of van den Berghe's argument would have to be evaluated through its application to comparative cases. However, the postulate of the primordiality of the 'ethny' seems to this writer excessively biologistic, and takes too literally the myths of common descent which are deployed rhetorically to bolster the ethnic ideology. The 'ethny' is, after all, a relational entity, its definition varying according to the opposition. Caste as an endogamous unit is characterized by ideological boundaries of common descent, thus marking off castes from each other. But common descent might also be invoked in a manner which transcends caste divisions to distinguish Hindu from Muslim, Buddhist or Sikh. As mentioned above, the ethnographic record overflows with instances of genealogical contrivances depicting a group as being of 'one blood', 'one house', or a clear traceable line, which may be changed or denied with just as much conviction when circumstances suggest that this may be politic.

While van den Berghe treats ethnicity as the fashionable evocation of primordial sentiment, Gellner sees it as anachronistic, arguing that its sentimental appeal is now weaker than that of a greater nationalism:

It is the large and effective units which seem natural, and it is their breakdown and fragmentation which is eccentric and requires special explanation. (Gellner, 1978, p. 133).

Indeed, he says, modern nationalist sentiments are particularly striking since they are often not the subject of contrivance and may even precede the formal creation of the national entity. Ironically, though, part of his explanation for the rise of nationalism resembles van den Berghe's for the primacy of the ethny: 'The call of blood or group loyalty or territoriality . . .' (Gellner, 1978, p. 142). Gellner maintains that what transfers the repository of these sentiments from ethny or small community to nation. is the nature of modern social structure: a complex division of labour which cuts across the elementary constituents of society. Van den Berghe would presumably respond that it is precisely because the solidarity of these other units is undermined by social and technological change that ethnicity remains a credible focus for social mobilization. It has been argued, for example, that the resurgence of ethnicity has followed from the decreasing saliency of class. The doctrine of 'liberal expectancy', promising equality or fair reward for all, is manifestly controverted by ethnic stratification (Burgess, 1978). The ethnically disadvantaged groups use the precedents offered by recent struggles for decolonization and Independence to press the integrity of their own claims (Burgess, 1978, p. 277). Elsewhere van den Berghe offers a similar explanation for the recent outburst of ethnic aspirations in Europe, which he portrays as, '. . . the last phase of imperial disintegration. If the Fiji Islands can be independent, why not Scotland?' (1976, p. 247).

The logic of Burgess's argument might also be extended to another aspect of modern governmental failure — *scale,* the very aspect which, for Gellner, renders ethnicity anomalous and anachronistic. As government becomes bigger and more remote form the constituent elements of society; as its economics appears to become increasingly centralized and institutionalized, so it loses credibility and relevance as a referent of people's identity. In Europe, the supra-national power of the EEC has made government seem even more remote from the regions than it was previously. The scale of such government means also that it has to operate either at an extraordinarily high level of generality or in response to very particular and powerful interests. In both cases, the vast majority of people are going to feel under-represented and inadequately understood. They may even feel deliberately excluded (cf. Smith, 1981). As a result, they become politically introspective and reach back to a more convincing level of society with which to identify (see, for examples, Beer, 1980; Boissevain, 1975, p. 14).

Here I think we are on firmer ground than with the over-theorized attempts to distinguish among ethnic, nationalistic or other collective sentiments. It is not our task to define ethnicity, but only to see if its various analyses offer us any clues to people's inclination to give primacy to their community memberships over their higher-scale attachments. Indeed, it may be that 'ethnicity' is so vague, and so variously used, a term that its definition can only be stipulative and arguments about its definition only sterile. We can make germane the contributions to the debate if we slightly alter their focus from the causes of 'ethnicity' to the generation of some form of sub-national, or sub-state, communal sentiment. We could then treat as empirical matters, for investigation in particular cases, the question of why the idiom of this sentiment is sometimes 'ethnic' and, in other cases, stresses some different sectionalism.

Proceeding in this way, we can reconcile all the speculations advanced in this discussion. Ethnicity, couched in the rhetoric of kinship, implies a degree of commonality sufficiently high to override intervening sectional interests in given situations. This commonality becomes increasingly persuasive since the 'higher level' claims of its obsolescence are manifestly unwarranted. It is a convincing level of sociality to contrast with the national and supra-national entities which are recognized increasingly as having failed to deliver the economic and political goods. This failure itself breeds another: the bankruptcy of the higher level entities as socio-psychological repositories of identity. To be Norwegian is only to be different from Swedes or Danes. To be a Norwegian Saami is to have a range of interests which, in discriminating you from 'white' Norwegians paints a much fuller portrait. To be a Saami in the Nuortabealli *s'iida* is to say almost everything of social significance about yourself, for it encompasses your kinship, your friendship, your domicile, your modes of life, love and death; it is the *whole* person. The suggestion is, then, that people assert community, whether in the form of ethnicity or of locality, when they recognize in it the most adequate medium for the expression of their whole selves.

Such recognition does not imply necessarily that people perceive an exact identity of interest between themselves and their community. It could simply be that the community provides them with a model for the political formulation of their interests and aspirations – a model which may have been provided unwittingly by authority at a higher echelon. The stimulus of de-colonization, mentioned above, would be an example. One observer has suggested that the government's recognition of certain 'official' Welsh interests, exemplified by the Welsh Office, the Welsh Tourist Board, and BBC Wales, provided devolutionist militants with paradigms for the further definition of sectional interests (Aull, 1978).

Another possibility, and one which directly addresses the view of symbolism which has been advanced here, is that 'community' provides not so much a model, but more an expedient medium for the expression of very diverse interests and aspirations. This is an approach which has been taken more generally to the phenomenon of social movements by the sociological historian, Charles Tilly. He sought an explanation of the Vendée, the counter-revolutionary movement in late eighteenth-century France, mistrusting the conventional imputation by historians of common motives to so vast a number of people. By careful analysis he finds the amorphous mass, 'counter-revolutionaries', to be composed of a sociological variety of components, to each of which distinctive motives could be attributed. He therefore suggests that a rigorous distinction has to be drawn by the analyst between the ideological rhetoric of the movement — say, its aims and aspirations as enunciated by its leaders — and the actual motivations of its individual members (Tilly, 1963; also 1974).

Tilly's argument is persuasive. It compels us to see the social movement as a kind of ideological hatstand — a single piece of furniture which, nevertheless, can accommodate a large number and wide variety of hats. The movement's programme may appear quite specific; yet, its component items are, like symbols themselves, amenable to idiosyncratic interpretation by the members in the light of their own circumstances and experiences. Thus, if we revert briefly to the example of Welsh nationalism, we can readily understand that the campaign for Welsh language rights, for the devolution of governmental powers, and for the restriction of English influence might mean very different things to the Pembrokeshire hill farmer, the academic historian in Aberystwyth, the slate miner in Blaenau and the farm worker in 'Llan' (see, for example, Emmett, 1964, 1982). Yet, they may all find in Plaid Cymru as an organization, or in Welsh nationalism as a cause, an articulate medium for their own, perhaps inchoate, sentiments. The movement and cause themselves become symbolic, condensing all the innumerable political grievances, ambitions, aspirations and propensities of its thousands of followers. It fills a vacuum; without it, these feelings would only be expressed in a highly fractionalized and ineffective way. Indeed, they should probably not be heard at all.

COMMUNITY AND IDENTITY

Whilst 'community' might not have the structure or direction which we associate with social movements, it may nevertheless serve a similar need. It is a largely mental construct, whose 'objective' manifestations in locality or ethnicity give it credibility. It is highly symbolized, with the consequence that its members can invest it with their selves. Its character is sufficiently malleable that it can accommodate all of its members' selves without them feeling their individuality to be overly compromised. Indeed, the gloss of commonality which it paints over its diverse components gives to each of them an additional referent for their identities.

So, to the question, 'why do communities respond assertively to encroachment upon their boundaries?', we can now speculate along the following lines. They do so because their members feel themselves to be under so severe a threat from some extrinsic source that if they do not speak out now they may be silenced for ever. Further, they do so because their members recognize their own voices within them, and because they feel the message of this vocal assemblage, though general, to be informed directly by their own experiences and mentalities. And they do so because their members find their identities as individuals through their occupancy of the community's social space: if outsiders trespass in that space, then its occupants' own sense of self is felt to be debased and defaced. This sense is always tenuous when the physical and structural boundaries which previously divided the community from the rest of the world are increasingly blurred. It can therefore easily be depicted as under threat: it is a ready means of mobilizing collectivity. Thus, one often finds in such communities the prospect of change being regarded ominously, as if change inevitably means loss. A frequent and glib description of what is feared may be lost is 'way of life'; part of what is meant is the sense of self.

This intimate relationship between community and identity has been described as 'cultural totemism' or 'ethnognomony' (Schwartz, 1975). These terms suggest that community, and its refraction through self, marks what is not, as well as what is, emphasizing traits and characteristics, 'at once emblematic of the groups's solidarity and of the group's contrasting identity and relation to the groups within its ambit of comparison' (Schwartz, 1975, p. 108). Such contrastive marking is exactly what makes the notion of 'boundary' so central to an understanding of community. Looking outwards across the boundary, people construct what they see in terms of their own stereotypes, this outward view forming a 'self-reflexive portion' of their culture (Schwartz, 1975), precisely the reflexivity which, as we noted earlier, Boon (1982) describes as a culture playing the *vis-à-vis*. We shall shortly touch on its association with the symbolic behaviour we have already encountered.

But in the context of our present discussion of the motivation of community assertiveness, we may note that this stimulus may not necessarily derive from any articulate and committed sense of the inherent character of a community; but, rather, from a felt need to discriminate it from some other entity. As van den Berghe suggests (see above) precedents may be of great importance as well, such assertions of distinctiveness resembling the domino theory of politics: once one group marks out its distinctiveness, others feel compelled to follow suit. In some cases, saliency attaches less to the *substance* of the supposed distinctiveness, and more to the need to display it. In this respect community is the compass of individual identity; it responds to the need to delimit the bounds of similarity. Without the benefit of hindsight, Durkheim thought this need would be swept away by the political and economic logic of large-scale systems of production. They would appear to have brought about almost the entirely opposite effect.

Case: Alcalá, again

Our conclusions regarding the saliency of contrast are well-illustrated in *People of the Sierra*, Pitt-Rivers's (1971) classic study of the Andalusian town of Alcalá, which we encountered briefly earlier in this essay. The ethos of community in Alcalá, as in other towns and villages of the Andalusian Sierra, is strongly informed by this contrastive sense. The Alcalareños, some three thousand in number, are clearly Andalusians — in dress, speech, provenance — and have a manifestly greater commitment to Andalusia than they have to the conceptually remote entity of Spain itself. Yet, the communities of the Sierra have a markedly developed sense of their differences from each other. These differences are not expressed neutrally but, rather, as denigration in abusive and satirical terms. The towns tend to be grouped in pairs, each 'twinned' with one regarded in Andalusia as most similar to it. Yet, it is the components of these pairs which loathe and revile each other more than they do the other communities of the region. Here we encounter once more a principle we have had occasion to note earlier: the finer the differences between people, the stronger is the commitment people have to them. Pitt-Rivers describes the animosity as follows:

> The sentiment of attachment to the pueblo is counterbalanced, as might be expected, by a corresponding hostility towards neighbouring pueblos. Thus, for the Alcalareño, those of Jacinas are boastful and false, those of Montejaque cloddish and violent, those of Benalurin are mean, those of El Jaral drunken and always drawing their knives . . . Each pueblo possesses a collection of ballads recording local history, and of sayings and rhymes in which the praises of the pueblo are sung and derogatory observations are made of its neighbours. (Pitt-Rivers, 1971, pp. 8–10)

And, he continues,

> It is always the people of the next-door town who are the
> cause of the trouble, who come stealing the crops, whose wives
> are unfaithful, who swear more foully, are more often drunk,
> more addicted to vice and who do one down in business. In
> all things they serve as a scapegoat or as a warning. (1971,
> p. 30).

This contrastive sense of the community feeds back also into its sense
of self. The quotation above refers to 'the sentiment of attachment to
the pueblo . . .' but this simple formula is revealed, on inspection, to
mask a marvellous complexity. The 'pueblo' denotes not only the territorial entity of the village, but also its social reality: its solidary spirit
and collective opinion. The pueblo, in this respect, is the people. But
all of the people? Well, only in so far as the village distinguishes itself,
or is distinguished from, other villages. The population of the village
is itself divided, although the nature of its divisions is somewhat elusive.

The most general division can be expressed as one between two
classes, the *señoritos,* and the *pueblo* – here, in its other guise, which
Pitt-Rivers renders as 'the plebs'. The señoritos are not easy to define in
structural terms. They number among themselves people who are
economically superior to the plebs, though this is not true of them all.
The señoritos are land-owners; but some plebs also own land. They are
merchants or shop-keepers, but may also supplement their incomes
through manual agricultural work. They include professionals, such as
the doctor, teacher and chemist, but these people also hold other positions. They are not gentry. They are not an hereditary class of economic
superiority, since property tends to be dispersed rather than consoli-
dated by the prevailing conventions of partible inheritance. Certainly,
their greater wealth does not, of itself, set them apart as a prestigious
elite. The señoritos are the vestiges of the patronal institution, although
not all of them accept the obligations of patronage. On the whole,
the señoritos tend to be more outward-looking than the plebs, identifying
to a greater extent with the world beyond the village. The plebs, by
contrast, are parochial, both in outlook and commitment.

So, the pueblo evinces a class-like division (although it is not,
strictly speaking, one of class) which is characterized by differences of
wealth, status and social universe. To its solidarity is also juxtaposed
the need for secrecy. The viability of economic life depends upon
evading the tax inspector whose scrutiny would otherwise make the
production of staples such as olive oil, bread and yarn financially im-
practicable. The natural intimacy of the pueblo makes the surrepti-

tious avoidance of the law extremely hazardous:

> People live very close to one another under conditions which make privacy difficult. Every event is regarded as common property and is commented on endlessly. (1971, p. 31)

Therefore, the successful practice of a deceit calls for the exercise of secrecy:

> To hide a secret from one person, it is better to hide it from all, while the less you tell the less chance there is of the true story being put together. . . . *Calla'ito* (on the quiet), it is explained, is how things are done here. . . . To give away information about your affairs puts you in a weak position, for you can no longer keep the other man guessing. (1971, p. 207)

This contradiction between solidarity and secrecy is capable of resolution, of course, for keeping one's mildly subversive activities secret avoids implicating other people in the misdemeanour. Such a resolution may appear theoretical. The practicalities of the situation are provided by the internal contradiction of those very principles which the pueblo emphasizes to distinguish itself from other communities. It is fiercely egalitarian — but shows class. It has a strong communality — but places a very high premium on privacy and secrecy. But these contradictions do not make the pueblo hypocritical in its collective self-image. Rather, the self-image energizes the theory and is, in turn, fuelled by it. The ideology of solidarity, in virtue of which the pueblo sees itself as a moral community, places a heavy emphasis on egalitarianism. This is what complicates the definition of the señoritos as a class. It also explains why wealth and prestige are not coincident. Wealth earns neither entitlement to respect nor access to power and influence. In Alcalá, it is held, the value of money does not lie in its possession, nor in its quantity: it inheres, rather, in the uses to which it is put (Pitt-Rivers, 1971, pp. 62–3).

Pitt-Rivers speaks of this ethic as 'the subjection of economic values to moral and social values'. In practice, these values are sufficiently imprecise that judgements founded on them can be adjusted to suit circumstances. The individual precedes the social category. You may invoke the ideology of charitableness to praise someone whom you wish to praise; someone else who has performed the same works but who, for whatever reason, is not held in the same kind of esteem, would not be accorded these plaudits. The whole paraphernalia of personal identity in Alcalá resonates with a similar logic. For example, the precedence of the individual over the category is evident in the greater currency of nicknames than of family names. But nicknames which might appear to be descriptively neutral are plainly not so:

> 'The Baker' is not a baker but a farmer. 'The Little Lame One' walks sound. 'The Toothless One' has all his teeth. 'The Bald One' all his hair. 'The Ugly One' is considerably better looking than 'The Pretty One'. (1971, p. 163).

Individuals are constituted socially by the stock of public knowledge; their intrinsic characteristics may be incidental, or even irrelevant (cf. Cohen, 1978). In this way, again, the judgement (for social identity *does* entail evaluation) is adjustable in the light of circumstances.

This flexibility of judgement is shown repeatedly in Pitt-Rivers's account of Alcalá. We have seen that no kudos attaches inherently to the possession of wealth. Rather, it is the application of wealth which earns prestige. Wealth, in and of itself, impugns the egalitarianism of the pueblo. *Los ricos,* the rich, are generally denigrated and are held to be responsible for the hardships of the poor: 'They have perverted the social order through their ambitions. They are the source of corruption' (1971, p. 62). As such a malign species, they clearly cannot be identified within the pueblo, whatever may actually be the disparities of wealth within the pueblo. *Los ricos*, then, are always from somewhere else: they are 'them' as opposed to 'us'. Should it happen that we find *un rico* in our midst (that is to say, not merely someone who is richer than the rest, but who flouts the moral code) we can manipulate his personal history to show that he is not really one of 'us' but originates from elsewhere. A similar malleability of judgement and category may be observed in the attribution of the honorific title 'Don'. It is evident that any abstracted set of rules for the 'honour' would collapse on application to specific cases. People of equivalent wealth, authority or power are treated quite dissimilarly in this regard, some being 'Don', but others not. The most that may be said with certainty is that the Don is different: he must be, for to distinguish him as Don is to mark him out from the pueblo. So, he is not one of 'us'. Even sons of the pueblo who achieve some eminence, but who continue to live in and like the pueblo, cannot be Don, 'because they are felt to be no different from others. They are part of the pueblo' (1971, p. 73).

The phenomenon we witness in Alcalá, and which is evident in many boundary-conscious communities (see, for example, Cohen, 1978), is as follows. The sense of community inheres in the putative and stereotypic differences between Alcalá and its neighbouring towns. But these differences, if not exactly fictions, are gross simplifications, since social life within Alcalá, as we should expect, has a complexity and diversity which belie the stereotype. Nevertheless, the stereotype constrains the expression of internal diversity by providing the vocabulary of values through which people construct their understanding of the social world. Thus, we have seen, for example, that the range of 'permissible' nicknames is limited to those which have local currency, resulting in some very arbitrary designations. We have seen also that Alcalá society manifests inequalities which contravene the stereotypic egalitarianism of the pueblo. Again, the differentiation is limited idiomatically — as in the categories 'señorito' and 'Don' — with idiosyncratic and inconsistent consequences. The principle is that the person precedes the category; principles are bent to the person, rather than the other way around. The shared *vocabulary* of value, not any orthodoxy of the values themselves, therefore enables the integrity of the community's self-image, and its sense of distinctive self, to be maintained. Following the argument of our earlier chapters, we can regard this vocabulary as having symbolic character and function, allowing people to share conceptual forms, without also requiring them to share their meanings. It provides them with the means to gloss over the innumerable factors which divide them in the course of day-to-day social life, in order to present themselves, by contrast with other communities, as having an essential likeness, for it is on this likeness that their solidarity is founded.

The Alcalareños are especially resourceful in limiting structural division. They make personality precede category; they make the voluntaristic relationships of friendship and of *compadrazgo* (ritual and fictive kinship) more important than the ascriptive ties of biological kinship. In so doing, of course, they complicate (rather than simplify) social differences, but in a way which leaves these contradictions amenable to a resolution based on their language of values — Alcalá culture. Each can make his or her own sense, but in terms shared with others. The variability thus engendered explains why Pitt-Rivers finds the social reality of Alcalá so hard to pin down, its rules so elusive, its exceptions so rife. For, as he cogently observes, social reality 'exists only in the minds' of Alcalá's members (1971, p. 208).

Our argument has been, similarly, that community is largely in the mind. As a mental construct, it condenses symbolically, and adeptly, its bearers' social theories of similarity and difference. It becomes an eloquent and collective emblem of their social selves.

OPPOSITION AND BOUNDARY: THE SYMBOLIC CONSTRUCTION OF COMMUNITY

As we have noted earlier, the sense of social self at the levels of both individuality and collectivity are informed by implicit or explicit contrast. Individuals are said to define themselves by reference to a 'significant other'; likewise, 'self-conscious' cultures and communities. In his recent book, *Other Tribes, Other Scribes,* the anthropologist James Boon has argued that the need to draw and express such contrasts provides the essential character of cultures. They only 'need' to formulate a sense of themselves as coherent and distinctive because they confront others. Moreover, just as other cultures are only observable from the perspective of a culture with which it is contrasted, so also people see their *own* culture from the supposed vantage point at which they imagine others to view it (1982, especially pp. 6, 25). Since the vitality of cultures lies in their juxtaposition, they exaggerate themselves and each other. Culture is thus inherently antithetical. In this respect cultures write large the character of their atomistic constituents, symbols, for by their very nature these too express contrast and distinction: 'Everything emerges as a contrastive replaceable for its complement . . .' (1982, p. 213), and, 'Every discourse, like every culture, inclines toward what it is not: toward an implicit negativity' (1982, p. 232).

Earlier in this book we saw instances in which the apparent contradiction of normality through symbolic means is used to draw attention to, and thereby to protect, the norm. We have also remarked on the symbolic demarcation of category divisions. All such phenomena manifestly incline towards 'an implicit negativity' — but since they *are* symbolic, and thus lack fixed and objective meanings, the negativity must always be contingent and never absolute. By the same token, the contrasts made by one culture with respect to another should not be thought of as absolute but, also, as contingent, as relational. Alcalareños may regard the pueblo of Jacinas as lacking every virtue on which they pride themselves, and as displaying every vice of which they see themselves as blessedly innocent. Yet, their sense of the virtuous may be founded conceptually on their perception of (and adjacency to) its opposite.

This contingency is the phenomenon celebrated by Dumont in his discussion of caste, as 'complementary opposition', in which the whole is founded upon the co-existence of juxtaposed parts. The co-membership of Mbuti pygmies and Bira villagers in *Nkumbi,* with which we began this chapter, is a case in point. This is not to view the whole in Hegelian (and Lévi-Straussian) terms as a reconciliation of opposites. Rather, as we saw in the first chapter, the idea is Durkheimian: that the whole is greater than, and subordinates (Dumont says (1980, p. 239) 'encompasses') the parts which take their character from it. Applying this principle to the community, we could say that it derives its sense of self from contrasting its self to others, but, further, from its juxtaposition with others in a larger relationship. For example, although for some purposes Alcalá and Jacinas measure themselves *against* each other, in respect of other purposes they may recognize themselves as more alike than different. As Andalusians, they may see in each other the virtues (or, at least, an approximation to them) which Castillans and Catalonians lack. Here, as in Evans-Pritchard's account of segmentation among the Nuer, the boundaries marking similarity and difference are not necessarily graduated, but may be drawn with regard to distinct referents.

This perspective also helps us to shed more light on the apparent inconsistency between social process *within* the community and *between* communities. for it makes intelligible the fact that, like the individual, the community may behave in quite different ways with respect to different 'significant others'. Like the individual, it may even behave differently to the same 'other' on different occasions. We should not have to regard such seemingly inconsistent behaviour as schizophrenic, nor as unprincipled. We may simply assume that the individual (or community) in question perceives the circumstances as differing in respects of which the other is unaware.

Further, we can apply this notion of complementarity to the 'classical' theories of community we touched on briefly in the first chapter. As we saw, the transitions from mechanical to organic solidarity; from *Gemeinschaft* to *Gesselschaft*; from traditionality to rational-legality; from status to contract, which are so often treated as theories of social change, evolution and development, might rather be seen as different modalities of behaviour *within* any society at any given period of its history. Thus, for example, mechanic solidarities (complementarily opposed to each other) exist *within* organic structures (say, the loyalty to each other of the first violins in opposition to the cellos). Durkheim recognized the historical compatibility of these supposedly opposite tendencies although he regarded the persistence of mechanical forms as a source of difficulty. He therefore advocated the necessity for a clear and unambiguous transformation through the restructuring of society. Weber also recognized their empirical mutuality, and, hence, described the contrasted states as mere 'ideal' types. Moreover, although he regarded this mutuality as 'irrational', he did not lament it as such, but only for its specific manifestations — as, for example, the survival of the Kaiser and Junkers into the 'modern' German era.

The significance of all this for our purposes is that the transformation supposedly wrought by these transitions has often been interpreted as rendering the community obsolete. The revision of this view, seeing the 'contrasting' states as co-existent, enables us to see the survival, the burgeoning, the *assertion* of community, not as an aberration to be explained, but as a normal, expectable expression of the resilience of culture: of people's sense of self. (It would probably take more than *one* kick on the shin to dissuade our supplicant dancer from ever approaching a girl again.) The process may be anathema to some powerful forces in modern society; but that may be to say only that it calls now to a greater extent than in the past on that sense of self and the ingenuity with which it may be expressed. Community, whether local or ethnic, or in whatever form, need not therefore be seen as an anachronism in urban–industrial society. Rather, it should be regarded as one of the modalities of behaviour available within such societies. That its symbolic expression is frequently in terms antagonistic to the larger society is a matter of interest, but not of pathology. It is simply an example of, what Dumont (1980) calls, 'the encompassment of the contrary' in complementary opposition.

As we have seen, the diminution of the geographical bases of community boundaries has led to their renewed assertion in symbolic terms. Since the boundaries are inherently oppositional, almost any matter of perceived difference between the community and the outside world can be rendered symbolically as a resource of its boundary. The community can make virtually anything grist to the symbolic mill of cultural distance, whether it be the effects upon it of some centrally formulated government policy, or a matter of dialect, dress, drinking or dying. The symbolic nature of the opposition means that people can 'think themselves into difference'. The boundaries consist essentially in the contrivance of distinctive meanings within the community's social discourse. They provide people with a referent for their personal identities. Having done so, they are then themselves expressed and reinforced through the presentation of those identities in social life. We have seen this with respect to the explicit allocation of identity — as, for example, in Alcalareño nicknaming, and in the assumption by Huichol *hikuritámete* of the personae of their gods — but also in more tacit processes of identity which rest solely upon communal knowledge, as evident among the people of Cat Harbour; the Utku Inuit; and the mourners of Modjokuto.

Our argument has been, then, that whether or not its structural boundaries remain intact, the reality of community lies in its members' perception of the vitality of its culture. People construct community symbolically, making it a resource and repository of meaning, and a referent of their identity.

References

Note. References preceded by an asterisk are particularly recommended for further reading.

Almond, G. & Verba, S. (1963) *The civic culture,* Boston: Little, Brown & Co.

Apter, A. (1983) 'In dispraise of the king: rituals "against" rebellion in south-east Africa', *Man* (N.S.) **18** (3), 521–534.

Apter, D. (1963) 'Political religion in the new nations', in C. Geertz (ed.), *Old Societies and new states: the quest for modernity in in Asia and Africa,* New York: Free Press of Glencoe.

Arensberg, C. & Kimball, S. (1965) *Culture and community,* New York: Harcourt, Brace & World.

Aull, C. (1978) *Ethnic nationalism in Wales: an analysis of the factors governing the politicisation of ethnic identity*, unpublished Ph.D. dissertation, Duke University.

Babcock, B. A. (1978) 'Introduction', in B. A. Babcock (ed), *The reversible world: symbolic inversion in art and society,* London: Cornell University Press, pp. 13–36.

Banfield, E. C. (1958) *The moral basis of a backward society,* New York: Free Press of Glencoe.

*Barth, F. (1969) 'Introduction', in F. Barth (ed.), *Ethnic Groups and boundaries: the social organisation of culture difference,* London: George Allen & Unwin, pp. 9–38.

Bateson, G. (1958) [1936] *Naven* (2nd edn.), Stanford: Stanford University Press.

Beer, W. (1980) *The unexpected rebellion: ethnic activism in contemporary France,* New York: New York University Press.

*Bell, C. & Newby, H. (1971) *Community studies,* London: George Allen & Unwin.

Benedict, M. & Benedict, B. (1982) *Men, women and money in Seychelles,* London: University of California Press.

Berghe, P. van den (1976) 'Ethnic pluralism in industrial societies: a special case?' *Ethnicity* **3**, 242–255.

Berghe, P. van den (1981) *The ethnic phenomenon,* New York: Elsevier.

Binns, C. (1979, 1980) 'The changing face of power: revolution and accommodation in the development of the Soviet ceremonial system' I, *Man* (N.S.) **14** (4), 585–606; II, *Man* (N.S.) **15** (1), 170–187.

Boissevain, J. (1975) 'Introduction: towards a social anthropology of Europe', in J. Boissevain & J. Friedl (eds.), *Beyond the community: social process in Europe,* The Hague: European-Mediterranean Study Group, University of Amsterdam, pp. 9–17.

*Boon, J. A. (1981) *Other tribes, other scribes: symbolic anthropology in the comparative study of cultures, histories, religions and texts,* Cambridge: Cambridge University Press.

Bouquet, M. (1981) *The sexual division of labour: the farm household in a Devon parish,* unpublished Ph.D. thesis, University of Cambridge.

*Briggs, J. (1970) *Never in anger: portrait of an eskimo family,* Cambridge, Mass.: Harvard University Press.

Brody, H. (1973) *Inishkillane: change and decline in the west of Ireland,* London: Allen Lane.

Burgess, M. E. (1978) 'The resurgence of ethnicity: myth or reality', *Ethnic & Racial Studies* **1** (3), 267–285.

Burridge, K. (1960) *Mambu, a Melenesian millenium,* London: Methuen.

Carlen, P. (1976) *Magistrates' justice,* London: Martin Robertson.

Chapman, M. (1982) ' "Semantics" and the "Celt" ', in D. J. Parkin (ed.), *Semantic anthropology,* London: Academic Press, pp. 123–143.

Cohen, Abner (1980) 'Drama and politics in the development of a London carnival', *Man* (N.S.) **15**.

Cohen, A. P. (1975) *The management of myths: the politics of legiti-*

mation in a Newfoundland community, Manchester: Manchester University Press.

Cohen, A. P. (1977) 'For a political ethnography of everyday life: sketches from Whalsay, Shetland', *Ethnos* 3—4, 180—205.

Cohen, A. P. (1978) '"The same — but different!" The allocation of identity in Whalsay, Shetland', *Sociological Review* 26 (3), 449—469.

Cohen, A. P. (1979) 'The Whalsay croft: traditional work and customary identity in modern times', in S. Wallman (ed.), *The social anthropology of work*, London: Academic Press, pp. 249—267.

Cohen, A. P. (1982a) 'Blockade: a case study of local consciousness in an extra-local event', in Cohen (1982c).

Cohen, A. P. (1982b) 'A sense of time, a sense of place: the meaning of close social association in Whalsay, Shetland', in Cohen (1982c).

*Cohen A. P. (1982c) *Belonging: identity and social organisation in British rural cultures*, Manchester: Manchester University Press.

Cohen, A. P. (1985) 'Symbolism and social change: matters of life and death in Whalsay, Shetland', *Man* (N.S.) 20 (2).

Cohen, A. P. & Comaroff, J. L. (1976) 'The management of meaning: on the phenomenology of political transactions', in B. Kapferer (ed.), *Transaction and Meaning*, Philadelphia: ISHI, pp. 87—107.

Cohen, P. S. (1969) 'Theories of myth', *Man* (N.S.) 4 (3), 337—353.

Cranston, M. (1954) *Freedom: a new analysis*, London: Longman.

Danforth, L. M. (1982) *The death rituals of rural Greece*, Princeton: Princeton University Press.

*Dore, R. (1978) *Shinohata: a portrait of a Japanese village*, New York: Pantheon.

Douglas, M. (1966) *Purity and danger: an analysis of concepts of pollution and taboo*, London: Routledge & Kegan Paul.

Du Boulay, J. (1982) 'The Greek vampire: a study of cyclic symbolism in marriage and death', *Man* (N.S.) 17 (2), 219—238.

Dumont, L. (1980) *Homo Hierarchicus*, (revd. edn.) Chicago: University of Chicago Press.

Durkheim, E. (1964) [1902] *The division of labour in society*, New York: The Free Press.

Dyck, N. (ed.) (1985) *Indigenous peoples and the nation-state: Fourth World politics in Canada, Australia and Norway*, St. John's: ISER.

Edelman, M. (1964) *The symbolic uses of politics*, Urbana: University of Illinois Press.

Eidheim, H. (1969) 'When ethnic identity is a social stigma', in Barth (1969).

Emmett, I. (1964) *A North Wales village*, London: Routledge & Kegan Paul.

Emmett, I. (1982) 'Place, community and bilingualism in Blaenau Ffestiniog', in Cohen (1982c), pp. 202–221.

Epstein, A. L. (1978) *Ethos and Identity: three studies in ethnicity*, London: Tavistock.

Evans-Pritchard, E. E. (1956) *Nuer religion*, Oxford: Oxford University Press.

Faris, J. (1972) *Cat Harbour: a Newfoundland fishing settlement*, St. John's: ISER.

Forsythe, D. (1984) 'Urban–rural migration and local development: an Orkney case', in J. C. Hansen *et al.* (eds.), *Centre–periphery: theory and practice*, Sogn og Fjordane Regional College.

Fortes, M. (1970) 'Time and social structure: an Ashanti case study', in M. Fortes, *Time and social structure*, London: Athlone Press, pp. 1–32.

Fox, R. (1982) 'Principles and pragmatics on Tory Island', in Cohen (1982c), pp. 50–71.

Frankenberg, R. (1957) *Village on the Border*, London: Cohen & West.

Geertz, C. (1966) 'Religion as a cultural system', in M. Banton (ed.), *Anthropological approaches to the study of religion*, London: Tavistock, pp. 1–46.

*Geertz, C. (1975a) 'Thick description: toward an interpretive theory of culture', in C. Geertz, *The interpretation of cultures*, London: Hutchinson, pp. 3–30.

Geertz, C. (1975b) [1959] 'Ritual and social change: a Javanese example', in Geertz (1975a), pp. 142–169.

*Geertz, C. (1975c) [1972] 'Deep play: notes on the Balinese cockfight', in Geertz (1975a), pp; 412–453.

Geertz, C. (1983) [1975] 'Common sense as a cultural system', in C. Geertz, *Local knowledge: further essays in interpretive anthropology*, New York: Basic Books, pp. 73–93.

Gellner, E. (1978) 'Scale and nation', in F. Barth (ed.) *Scale and social organisation*, Oslo: Universitetsforlaget, pp. 133–149.

Gilsenan, M. (1976) 'Lying, honour, and contradiction', in B. Kapferer (ed.), *Transaction and meaning*, Philadelphia: ISHI, pp. 191–219.

Gluckman, M. (1962) 'Les rites de passage', in M. Gluckman (ed.) *Essays on the ritual of social relations*, Manchester: Manchester University Press, pp. 1–52.

Gluckman, M. (1963) [1952] 'Rituals of rebellion in south east Africa', in M. Gluckman, *Order and rebellion in tribal Africa*, London: Cohen & West, pp. 110–136.

Goffman, E. (1963) *Stigma*, Penguin: Harmondsworth.

Goffman, E. (1967) *Interaction ritual*, New York: Anchor Books.

Hanrahan, P. J. (1979) *Communities on the periphery*, unpublished M.A. thesis, University of Manchester.

*Helias, P.-J. (1979) *The horse of pride: life in a Breton village*, New Haven: Yale University Press.

Henriksen, G. (1973) *Hunters in the Barrens: the Naskapi on the edge of the white man's world*, St. John's: ISER.

Hillery, G. A. Jr. (1955) 'Definitions of community: areas of agreement', *Rural Sociology*, **20**.

Hodgkin, T. (1964) 'The relevance of "Western" ideas for the new African states', in J. R. Pennock (ed.), *Self-government in modernising nations*, Englewood Cliffs, N.J.: Prentice-Hall, pp. 50–80.

Humphrey, C. (1983) *Karl Marx Collective: economy, society and religion in a Siberian collective farm*, Cambridge: Cambridge University Press.

Kluckhohn, C. (1962) 'The concept of culture', in R. Kluckhohn (ed.), *Culture and behaviour*, New York: Free Press, pp. 19–73.

Ladurie, E. Le Roy (1980) *Montaillou*, Harmondsworth: Penguin.

Larsen, S. Saugestad (1982a) 'The two sides of the house: identity and social organisation in Kilbroney, Northern Ireland', in Cohen (1982c), pp. 131–164.

Larsen, S, Saugestad (1982b) 'The Glorious Twelfth: the politics of legitimation in Kilbroney', in Cohen (1982c), pp. 278–291.

Larsen, T. (1983) 'Negotiating identity: the Micmac of Nova Scotia', in A. Tanner (ed.), *The politics of Indianness*, St. John's: ISER, pp. 37–136.

Lawrence, P. (1964) *Road belong Cargo*, Manchester: Manchester University Press.

*Leach, E. R. (1954) *Political systems of highland Burma*, London: G. Bell & Son.

Leech, E. R. (1968) 'Introduction', in E. R. Leach (ed.), *The structural study of myth and totemism*, London: Tavistock, pp. vii–xix.

Lévi-Strauss, C. (1963) 'The structural study of myth', in *Structural anthropology*, New York: Basic Books.

Leyton, E. (1974) 'Opposition and integration in Ulster', *Man* (N.S.) **9**, 185–198.

Lienhardt, R. G. (1961) *Divinity and experience*, London: Oxford University Press.

Littlejohn, J. (1972) 'Temne right and left: an essay on the choreography of everyday life', in R. Needham (ed.), *Right and left*, London: University of Chicago Press, pp. 288–298.

McClelland, D. C. (1966) 'The impulse to modernization', in M. Weiner (ed.), *Modernization: the dynamics of growth*, New York: Basic

Books, pp. 28–39.

McFarlane, G. (1981) 'Shetlanders and incomers: change, conflict and emphasis in social perspectives', in L. Holy & M. Stuchlick (eds.), *The structure of folk models,* London: Academic Press, pp. 119–136.

Matthews, D. R. (1970) *Communities in transition,* unpublished Ph.D. dissertation, University of Minnesota.

Mewett, P. G. (1982) 'Exiles, nicknames, social identities and the production of local consciousness in a Lewis crofting community', in Cohen (1982c), pp. 222–246.

*Myerhoff, B. G. (1974) *Peyote hunt: the sacred journey of the Huichol Indians,* Ithaca: Cornell University Press.

Needham, R. (1979) *Symbolic classification,* Santa Monica: Goodyear Publishing.

Okely, J. (1975) 'Gypsy women: models in conflict', in S. Ardener (ed.), *Perceiving women,* London: Dent, pp. 55–86.

Oz, A. (1983) *In the land of Israel,* London: Fontana.

Pahl, R. (1968) 'The rural–urban continuum', in R. E. Pahl, (ed.), *Readings in urban sociology,* Oxford: Pergamon, pp. 263–305.

Paine, R. P. B. (1977) 'Tutelage and ethnicity, a variable relationship', in R. P. B. Paine (ed.), *The White Arctic: anthropological essays on tutelage and ethnicity,* St. John's: ISER, pp. 249–263.

Paine, R. P. B. (1982) *Dam a river, damn a people?* IWGIA Document, 45, Copenhagen: IWGIA.

Paine, R. P. B. (1985) 'Norwegians and Saami: nation-state and Fourth World', in G. Gold & R. P. B. Paine (eds.), *Mother country and ethnicity,* St. John's: ISER.

Park, R. (1925) 'The city: suggestions for the investigation of human behaviour', in R. Park *et al., The city,* Chicago: University of Chicago Press.

Peters, E. L. (1984) 'The paucity of ritual among Middle Eastern pastoralists', in A. S. Ahmed & D. M. Hart (eds.), *Islam in tribal societies,* London: Routledge & Kegan Paul, pp. 187–221.

Phillips, S. K. (1984) *Identity, social organisation and change: Muker parish, a Yorkshire dales community,* unpublished D.Phil. thesis, University of Oxford.

*Pitt-Rivers, J. A. (1971) *The people of the Sierra* (2nd Edn.), Chicago: Chicago University Press.

Rapport, N. J. (1983) *Are meanings shared and communicated? A study of the diversity of world views in a Cumbrian village,* unpublished Ph.D. thesis, University of Manchester.

Redfield, R. (1955) *The little community,* Stockholm: Almquist &

Wiksells Boktrycker.

Sallnow, M. J. (1981) 'Communitas reconsidered: the sociology of Andean pilgrimage', *Man* (N.S.) **16** (2), pp. 163–182.

Schneider, D. M. (1980) *American kinship: a cultural account* (2nd edn.), Chicago: University of Chicago Press.

Schwartz, T. (1975) 'Cultural totemism: ethnic identity primitive and modern', in G. De Vos & L. Romanucci-Ross (eds.), *Ethnic identity: cultural continuities and change,* Palo Alto: Mayfield, pp. 106–131.

Schwimmer, E. (1972) 'Symbolic competition', *Anthropologica* XIV (2), pp. 117–155.

Smith, A. D. (1981) *The ethnic revival in the modern world,* Cambridge, Cambridge University Press.

*Sperber, D. (1975) *Rethinking symbolism:* Cambridge: Cambridge University Press.

Stein, M. (1964) *The eclipse of community,* Princeton: Princeton University Press.

*Strathern, A. M. (1981) *Kinship at the core,* Cambridge: Cambridge University Press.

Strathern, A. M. (1982a) 'The place of kinship: kin, class and village status in Elmdon, Essex', in Cohen (1982c), pp. 72–100.

Strathern, A. M. (1982b) 'The village as an idea: constructs of village-ness in Elmdon, Essex', in Cohen (1982c), pp. 247–277.

Tilly, C. (1963) 'The analysis of a counter-revolution', *History & Theory* **III**.

Tilly, C. (1974) 'Foreword', in A. Blok, *The Mafia of a Sicilian village,* Oxford: Blackwell.

Turnbull, C. (1961) *The forest people,* London: Chatto & Windus.

Turnbull, C. (1983) *The Mbuti pygmies: change and adaptation,* New York: Holt, Rinehart & Winston.

Turner, R. H. (1962) 'Role-taking: process versus conformity', in A. M. Rose (ed.) *Human behaviour and social processes,* London: Routledge & Kegan Paul, pp. 20–40.

Turner, V. W. (1967) *The Forest of symbols,* Ithaca: Cornell University Press.

Turner, V. W. (1969) *The ritual process,* London: Routledge and Kegan Paul.

Wadel, C. (1973) *Now, whose fault is that? The struggle for self-esteem in the face of chronic unemployment,* St. John's: ISER.

Warner, W. (1984) *Distant water,* Harmondsworth: Penguin.

Weber, M. (1948) [1918] 'Politics as a vocation', in H. Gerth & C. Wright Mills (eds.), *From Max Weber,* London: Routledge & Kegan

Paul, pp. 77–128.

*Whyte, W. F. (1955) *Street corner society* (2nd edn.), Chicago: University of Chicago Press.

Wilson, B. (1967) 'The Pentecostalist minister', in B. Wilson (ed.), *Patterns of sectarianism*, London: Heinemann, pp. 138–157.

Wirth, L. (1951) [1938] 'Urbanism as a way of life', in P. K. Hatt & A. J. Reiss (eds.), *Cities and society*, New York: Free Press, pp. 46–63.

Worsley, P. M. (1964) *The third world*, London: Weidenfeld & Nicholson.

Worsley, P. M. (1967) *The trumpet shall sound* (2nd edn.), London: Paladin.

Worsley, P. M. (1984) *The three worlds: culture and world development*, London: Weidenfeld & Nicholson.

Index

Christianity p. 56 60 p.